Friends

forever

A He-Said She-Said Dating Story

Jim and Vicki Smith

xulon PRESS

Table of Contents

Chapter One

Breaking Up is Hard

⎯⎯⎯⎯⎯

We all want friends. Somehow in dating, we forget that we are friends. Some people don't even think about taking the time to get to know one another as friends before they start to date. They just let their hormones take control and forget that this "other person" is a human being with feelings and opinions that need to be honored. We become very selfish and only want what is best for "me", instead of what also is good for the other person. If we remember in our dating situations that we are responsible as "friends" to one another, we may become more careful in how we treat one another. However, even in the best of dating, there are times where one may not feel as attracted to the other or timing is off and one needs to break that "close friendship" that has been developed. That is what makes breaking up hard to do and when you date, there is always the possibility that a "break-up" or a "tearing apart" will happen. In our dating relationship, both of us went through a "break-up" of someone special in our lives, not knowing what God had around the corner. There is something to remember. Even though breaking up is hard to do, it prepares you for what is next. Always trust God, and yet treat one another as "friends" because you never know, this next relationship may be a "forever friend"!

Dating is an experience that is filled with thrills and spills. It's a little like military boot camp, allowing us to become a better person, but in the process, it exposes many of our weaknesses and shortcomings. If we are willing to be honest with ourselves, open enough to learn a few things about being with other people, dating can develop a person into a stronger, more mature and caring individual. It is never easy, and each person has different experiences that they must go through as they grow and mature.

Many dating relationships end without a marriage proposal. The average person seriously dates about 3-5 people before finding the person he wants to marry. That means that when you start out with a relationship, although you may not want to think about this, you most likely will have to go through a tough break-up, and breaking up is hard to do.

This is our story.

I quickly walked through the lobby and into the elevator. I pushed the button for the tenth floor and anxiously waited for the doors to close. Hopefully no one would join me in the elevator. I was granted my wish and as the doors closed, I found myself alone . I was frustrated. An angry moan escaped from my mouth. I pounded my fist against the wall and shouted to God, "why?"

The doors opened and I headed for my dorm room, not wanted to see anyone. Making my way down the hall, I slipped into my darkened room and shut the door. My room-mate was not coming back for several hours, so I had plenty of time to sort things out.

Totally overwhelmed and feeling absolutely helpless and alone, I fell to my knees and did what I should of done long ago, I prayed. I prayed for an explanation and for a solution.

Why did my girlfriend of fourteen months break up with me? I couldn't understand her reasoning, plus it was a blow to my ego. What was wrong with me? I didn't want this pain and I didn't want any lessons to be learned. Why was this happening?

I was never the dating kind of guy. Girls were a sure out on the softball team or an easy home run if they were playing against you in the outfield, so they never made a good impression on me. I loved athletic events, so if girls could not play or understand sports, I never took time to be with them. Plus, they always seemed to talk and giggle forever and that usually made me feel out of place and insecure. I thought they were talking about me and laughing at the way I walked, dressed or that I had lettuce stuck between my teeth.

I did like a girl in kindergarten, and I think she kissed me on the cheek once, but that relationship lasted only a day or so. In 5th grade, there was another girl in my life. We went to the same school and church, but we never talked. In fact, even when we supposedly were an item, we hardly ever talked. Instead, we exchanged notes and had a "middle person" who wrote all the notes like, "do you love, like or hate her? Check one of the above." I saved all these notes and hid them in my sock drawer. This all came to a screeching halt when I came home from school and discovered that my mom had cleaned my sock drawer, and the notes were gone! How embarrassing! I never did ask about those notes.

I also took a pretty girl in my church youth group to a high school banquet in high school, but that was about it. I really didn't start dating until the summer before my senior year in high school. It was a summer romance at a camp. We talked, laughed and went out with other staff members throughout the summer, but I never kissed her until the day she was going home. I went to say goodbye to her before she got to the parking lot where her parents were waiting. I was too shy to meet her parents, but I wanted to kiss her. We said our final goodbyes, and then I did it, but I almost missed her mouth. It was one of the little kisses you give your aunt, so I quickly tried again. This time I landed one right on the mouth. It was quick, but it left a strange sensation in my lips. They were tingling. I later told my friend about this sensation and he just laughed and dubbed me with the nickname "hot lips." The name was far from the truth, but they did tingle. We did not see each other much after the summer, so the relationship died out, but that wasn't even close to the hurt I felt after this breakup.

We started dating during my senior year in high school, and now we were freshmen in college. Maybe it hurt more now because we spent so much time together. Maybe it hurt because I thought we were going to last forever. What a mistake it was to assume we would last forever. I had looked to the future without paying attention to the present. Don't believe it until you are married. Even engagements don't mean you will get married.

I did not realize it then, but I was young and immature in the aspect of dating. My relationship was marked with jealousy, possessiveness, physical attraction and insecurity. I would sometimes call her, and if I received a busy tone, I would get jealous, thinking she was talking to someone else. I never liked her standing around with other guys either. I spent most of my time with her and less and less time with my friends. We knew how to kiss, but our relationship was weak in other areas. It was time to break up, but I was not ready. She tried to break up with me two months earlier, but I managed to convince her that we could work it out. I was scared that I would never find another girlfriend, afraid I would always be alone. Like the song says, breaking up is hard to do. It is easier to break up with someone, than being "dumped," and I was being "dumped." God answered my prayer to heal our relationship, but it was not the answer I wanted. He said no, and it was time to move on.

It was so cold, so quiet, and so grey. The air was heavy. I could see my breath, panting, as I tried to walk faster and faster, almost trying to run away from the reality of his words. "He couldn't have really meant what he said" came through one ear, but in the other came the stark darkness of a true ending, a chapter absolutely closed and not to be reopened again! I had never heard him use this closing tone of voice, this calm intellectual reasoning that cut through my heart. I kept telling myself with every step towards home that he would come back to me, that he needed me. He would be sorry and tomorrow everything would be back to normal. However, I seemed to be trying to persuade myself of this story, yet knowing deep inside that truly it was over and he was finished with "normal". "Normal" had only become few good times with more arguing and unhappiness for actually both of us, I thought, and he had the courage to finally start new lives for the both of us, but oh how it hurt! It shouldn't have been him, I should have done it, even done it long ago. What month was it? Oh, yes, I had known last July, but here it was January of the next year and I still hadn't obeyed. Obeyed who? That's all part of my story and must be told. All I knew now was that this pain was awful...it was cold, quiet and so grey inside as well as outside.

There was my house, finally just ahead. I walked through the door, straight to my room, fell onto my bed and stopped. A "good-bye" is very hard even when it is supposed to be a "goodbye". My heart seemed empty, fearful to be alone again, betrayed by the one whom I thought knew and loved me best. And then it happened. The sun shone through the window upon my head. That one ray seemed to be sent by God, the warmth and brightness in the midst of the coldness and grey. He seemed to say, "That's it Vicki. I'm really the only one who truly knows you and loves you. Let me completely fill your heart."

"O.K."I replied, weakly. This seemed to change my whole frame of mind.

What a simple answer to an overwhelming proposition, a proposition from THE all powerful , all knowing God. The answer allowed me to relax and finally put EVERY THING into my Master's hands. In this answer, I totally gave in to His direction. It was His answer, even if I didn't know all the reasons why or what all the plans ahead entailed.

However I should have submitted a long time ago, for I already had given this area to the Lord, but I guess I had taken it back again, only to botch it up.

"Please help me Lord. I've made such a mess of things. I wanted to do it your way but my own pride got in the way. I 'm so tired of trying to make everything work out my way. I truly want your way Lord!"

What had happened in my life that I was at this place? My intentions were so good. I remember it had all started when I was fifteen at camp....

Oh yes, church camp...what a great week...There was a speaker there that week who spoke on love, sex, and dating. I was writing down all the principles and learning a lot. I had a beautiful counselor that week, who was praying for her future mate and she hadn't even met him yet. What a great idea! From that moment on in July, I made a commitment to the Lord to pray in faith for my future mate at least once a week. Now, to make this very personal and a seirous commit-ment, I had two rules about this time spent in prayer: First of all, I told the Lord I would never pray for a future mate by name, and presume to tell God who my mate would be. Instead, I would always pray for the man who YOU will have me to marry. This way I couldn't just fill in the boyfriend's name whom I was dating at the time...even when I was engaged. I never used my fiancé's name. Always wanting God to have the final word!

Secondly, I vowed to the Lord that I wouldn't tell any other "guy" about this commitment of prayer for my future mate until I could personally share with my new husband that I had been praying for him. This didn't cheapen my vow by using it to try to impress a guy. It was a very personal vow between my Lord and I. Now,, to make a list of qualities that I wanted in my "husband to be."

First on my list, I wanted him to be a Christian, obviously. The Bible says to be "not unequally yoked, but to be of the same mind. However, I found that to some of my girlfriends, this didn't even seem to be important. They were just dating "any" boy, not asking or even caring whether they were a Christian or not. Not only is it smart to marry someone who has the same Godly views and values, but it also it is just being obedient to what the Lord has commanded us as His children. Of course, a lot of girls were glad that their boyfriends " said" they were a Christian. The problem was they didn't really take a look at the boy's Christian walk or character. In fact, many of the boys were worse than some who didn't even claim to be a Christian! So, next on my list, was that my future mate must not only CLAIM he is a Christian, but he is a GROWING Christian that showed leadership in following Christ. I wanted him to love God's Word and to know it well and be following His word.

Before I came up with the next qualities, I did some major research. You see, I always wondered how people knew who they were to marry, especially since some people would seem so sure and then end up in divorce. Also, I would watch many Christian marriages in church and how they treated or didn't treat each other and decided that I didn't really want to have a marriage like that. I decided that I needed to do some research by studying God's word and questioning some married couples about their marriages. I would ask them how they knew they were to marry the person they married. Their answer, no matter what age, personality or income would always be, "Well, you just know ...there's something in you that you just KNOW!" This just didn't make sense to me, especially since some people obviously DIDN'T seem to know. For some people, they obviously DIDN'T seem to know since there seemed to be many unhappy marriages and divorces. There had to be a better test or way to make your decision. So I went to God's word searching what God had to say about marriage and/or singleness.

Here ARE my conclusions:

Actually, in I Corinthians 7, God tells us that it is better that we remain single than to be married, for then we can give ourselves wholeheartedly to God's work and not have to concern ourselves with things of this world...however, it also says that if we cannot control ourselves, it is not wrong that we marry. In fact, He said, " It is better to marry than to burn." I realized that if God wanted you to marry, He believed that the two people together could glorify Him better together than they could alone. God's major purpose is to be glorified through our lives! That's it! The major purpose was that in marriage the two of you could glorify God together BETTER than you could alone!

We are the temple of God, housing the Holy Spirit. Now, if two of us were brought together, we would still be forming a temple of God for the Holy Spirit to shine through together. Therefore, wouldn't it be great if your "partner to be" would already have a couple fruits of the Holy Spirit strong in their life? Then, if you have developed some other fruits in your own life, the two of you would already start with some wonderful strengths at the time of your marriage. Here's what I mean. If my marriage was going to glorify God, I wanted it to be filled with the fruit of the Spirit. Look at Galatians 5:22-23 where it says, "But the fruit of the Spirit is love, joy, peace, patience, kindness, goodness, faith, gentleness and

*self-control...” You see, if you're filled with the Spirit, you
are to be producing these characteristics in your life all the
time so all praise goes to Jesus. Then I thought, “Wouldn't it
be great if your marriage portrayed these so the Lord Jesus
would actually be seen in your marriage every day!”*

*Now, when we read this verse, there are usually two of
the fruits that BOUNCE OUT at you right away because
you know that your life is far from showing these two
characteristics...(my two were faith and patience...I was an
only child, so my PATIENCE was nil because I always got
my way and there were no siblings to share with. I felt I had
no FAITH because I had pretty much received whatever I
needed or wanted. I felt that I never had these fabulous experiences of faith where God provided these miracles, JUST in
the nick of time with JUST what I had asked. I had always
heard missionaries tell these kind of great testimonies and
mistakenly felt that this was FAITH.)*

*Anyway, I thought, “Wouldn't it be great if my' partner
to be' exhibited these TWO fruits of faith and patience
ALREADY in his life?”*

*I ALSO realized that I had two fruits that were more
prevalent in my life that I could be developing with the Lord.
(I thought these two more prevalent fruits in my life were
LOVE and JOY. I really loved people and usually liked to
make people happy, or people always called me an optimist.)
If I studied these two Holy Spirit inspired fruits in my life
and looked for my future mate to have built into his life the
two fruits that I needed to work on, we would already have a
head start at the beginning of our marriage with 4 out of the
9 fruits to build upon. They say that you become more and
more like your partner as you spend life with them, so we
would rub off on each other and have a great start at glori-
fying God together!!!*

*Now I don't know if you got all that, but I was really
excited about this. My list so far consisted of:*

A Christian who is GROWING in his faith
Leadership
FAITH and PATIENCE being obvious in his life

This gave me a great start on how to pray for my future mate also. I would pray that the Lord would be producing leadership and growth in his life and carving out the Holy Spirit's fruit of Faith and Patience so I would learn from him and would someday realize that this was the one that God was preparing for me. (Hmm, do you think that is faith???)

I know that God doesn't make just one person for one other person, but I do believe that God is interested in who you marry. I really feel, besides your eternal salvation, your marriage partner is one of the most important decisions on earth you must make in your lifetime. It can help to make you or break you. However, now looking back on all of this, God did more than specifically answer my prayer for a husband. He taught me to pray specifically and be faithful in my prayers for someone else. He gave me an exercise in faith (praying for someone I hadn't even met or seen.) Finally, He taught me to pour into HIS work and grow in HIM. I used a concordance for the next two years to look up every verse that had something to do with "love" or "joy" in it. What a great study for a high school student and did I ever learn a lot!!

Now, I don't want you to think I was too super spiritual or too boring. I did happen to list a few other qualities I wanted: good-looking, cute,

> *likes to tease and joke around and have fun*
> *didn't always care about what others thought*
> *likes to have good, clean fun*
> *play a musical instrument (perhaps guitar)*
> *likes to sing*
> *likes sports and be pretty good at them (don't want to brag but I was pretty athletic and I do love sports probably thanks to my dad!)*

At the end of my list, I wrote a letter to God and it went
something like this:

Dear Lord,

*I really love You and believe that You are preparing
someone just for me, so that together we can serve You and
glorify You through a home run by You. I don't ever want
to tell You who I will marry...instead I want You to show
him to me kind of like You showed Abraham's servant when
You brought him Rebekah. I truly believe You will bring us
together in Your timing so help us both to wait upon You, give
us patience to wait through our teen years. Yes, Lord, please
help him to save himself for only me so that on our wedding
night we can present ourselves to one another pure, the way
You want marriage to be. Please help him to say no to temptation, to know that there is someone, someday who is going
to love him for who he is. If he is hurting because someone
has broken up with him, help him to cling to You and trust in
You. Help him to grow into a Godly man, a man who knows
and follows only what You ask of him, not what the world
wants of him. Please protect him and guide him in all of his
choices whether big ones or small ones. Thank you Lord.*

Vicki Sutter

*With that, I dated the letter, closed up my letter, went
home from camp and started to pray diligently. I prayed
every day the first few weeks, but always God reminded me
once a week to pray for this man of faith and patience. (If I
hadn't prayed for him by Saturday night, I would pray that
night, because Saturday night was usually date night, so
whether I had a date or not, I would pray for this one God
was preparing for me.)*

So with all this research and commitment on this subject, why was I here, lying on my bed, crying my eyes and heart out, having to say "YES" to God again? Because I'm only human, but God is God and He was answering my prayer... just in a whole different way than I would think. You see in Isaiah 55:8 -9, it says, "For my thoughts are not your thoughts , neither are your ways my ways, declares the Lord. As the heavens are HIGHER than the earth, so are MY ways HIGHER than your ways and MY thoughts than your thoughts."

Oh yes, God is God and His way will be!!

"In this world you will have trouble. But take heart!
I have overcome the world." John 16:33

Life is not always easy, and yet God is able to use all of our experiences for His glory and honor. Jesus had tough times, and ultimately died on the cross, even though he never did anything wrong. You will have tough days, rough experiences, and relation-ships that do not work out. Don't give up, don't quit; keep on struggling through those difficult times. He can take every experience we go through and turn it into something good.

Chapter Two

First Impressions

∽

Have you ever been going through your day, not expecting anything out of the ordinary to happen and then, suddenly, something happens that will change your life? I once was out mowing my yard when I received a phone call. That phone call was from someone I had never met, but it was a job offer that would soon have my family moving to another state. Every day of our lives can be like that. When we least expect it, someone may walk into our lives who will become a very special part of our lives. We never know what to expect, and yet we should never underestimate what one moment in our lives can do. Always be prepared for opportunities that you may encounter each and every day.

It is always amazing, how for weeks, months at a time you live out your life and meet many different people but then all of a sudden, in one moment, you meet that ONE person who takes your breath away or commands your curiosity or interest. They call it "attraction"! Those "first moments" give you memories for a lifetime and influence you forever. You never know when that "first impression" will be the one that changes your life. You never really know which door you walk through will be the one that opens up a whole new "door" into your life. A door to a "forever friend"...

Our story....

Okay God, Your ways are not my ways but what kind of way was this, God? Not only had my 16 month relationship with the only neat Christian guy in my town been broken up, but I heard the rumor that he liked one of my friends (also a great Christian girl) and now my face looked like a chipmunk, because I had just gotten my wisdom teeth pulled out! This was the pits!! Oh yeah, also in one week, I was going to have to get in front of a few hundred people and sing in my Youth for Christ singing group named, "The Reachouts" for a College career Day at a church in Peoria. I was sure I'd be the laughing stock of the day, "the girl" with the chipmunk cheeks! Oh well, it's just one day in my life, what big or exciting thing could happen anyway? My life was now ruined and boring, oh yeah, remember God's way?

Driving down to Peoria was a very long trip, but at least it was something to do on this particular Saturday. I would have otherwise stayed in my dorm room and sulked over my broken relationship. My boss Ken, who was also one of my sponsors in my youth group when I was in high school, was accompanying me on this trip. He knew that I had a pretty serious relationship going on, but while we talked, I never mentioned that we had just broken up. In fact, I never talked about girls at all during the three hour trip.

Ken did talk about the upcoming college fair we were going to at Grace Presbyterian Church in Peoria. This was a large church and it was expecting to host approximately six hundred high school students coming to check out the Christian College of their choice. Not only were we there, representing Moody, but several other schools were there in hope of encouraging many students to apply to their school. My job was to be the student representative from Moody, to give the students perspective. However, I was not feeling particularly excited about anything at the moment. Moody seemed to be a great place to break up, if that's what you enjoyed in life.

When we arrived, Ken and I registered and were assigned to a room to set up our Moody display. As the day progressed, I began to realize that the expected six hundred students were not going to show up, and although about two hundred did come, with so many colleges there, it would be a slow day in the display area for us.

We arrived at the church in the morning in time to set up to sing in the auditorium. After all the equipment was set up and the sound checks and practicing was completed, our director said we had the rest of the morning to walk around and look at the different college booths if we wanted to. My two friends had no idea where to go, but I knew immediately what booth I wanted to see. The bright spot in my future was my acceptance into Moody Bible Institute. I had dreamt of going there almost all my life and especially after my mission trip to the Dominican Republic and Haiti just after my Junior year in high school.

Sure enough, the day dragged on. A few students popped their heads into the room, but basically, it was a disappointment. As Ken and I were sitting in the room watching the paint fade, lo and behold, three students walked into the room. Now this was looking like the day might not be a total waste. Not only did these three students come into our room and brighten up our day by just breaking the monotony, these three students were girls! They were all attractive, however, one seemed a little too tall and one seemed a little too small for me, but one of them was just right. Her smile was contagious and immediately brightened my day. Her eyes sparkled with sincerity and understanding. She was so full of life and energy that whatever I was thinking before she came into the room suddenly vanished and my only thought was on how I might get to know this girl better. I didn't want to seem too obvious, so I remained somewhat reserved on the outside, while fireworks were going off inside my head!

Two good looking guys were at the booth, especially the one on the left. He had a great big smile that would make anyone feel welcome, shining beautiful dark brown eyes that swallowed me up, perfect blondish-brown hair, and a handsome high cheeked face with a masculine mustache. No boys in my high school had a mustache, so he must be an older college guy. Did I look too hard? Was I staring at this awesome guy? What was he saying? Oh yeah, sit down.

Immediately it was as if we were the only two in the room. Our eyes locked into place and he proceeded to answer all my questions and tell me everything anyone would want to know about Moody. He was so smart and so nice and so talkative, with a touch of teasing and yet so sincere to let me know all of Moody's rules so I would be ready for the school. It was so nice of him to prepare me, no wonder he was on the public relations staff. He knew everything, and he personified in my mind the great typical Moody student and was eager to be helpful and patient in explaining everything!

"Jim Smith" was his name and he was in his second semester at Moody. Wow! If all the guys at Moody were like this, I was going to be in for a treat, but he was so much older and more mature than me.

She introduced herself as Vicki Sutter and added that she had already been accepted to Moody for the fall semester.

She had come to find out some details about what it was like to be a student at Moody.

"This is great," I thought. We didn't have to promote Moody with the usual presentation. Ken looked at me and said, "Well, Jim is a student at Moody right now so why don't I let him do all the talking." All right Ken, I thought, thanks!

I thought I would have some fun and maybe stretch the truth a little. Vicki asked about dorm life and I, in my most sincere sounding voice and honest looking face, lied. I said dorm life was solely fro studying. I explained that my room-mate and I studied between five and six hours a night. We hardly ever talked and there were quiet hours from six at night until eight the next morning. Even if you wanted to talk, you weren't allowed to speak. Silence ruled the dorm. A resident assistant walks around the dorm floor to make sure you were quiet and studying. They would also provide assistance with your homework if you needed any help. I did mention that there was a study break from 10:00 - 10:30pm, which we all appreciated, but basically dorm life was full of serious studying.

Ken was letting the joke continue and Vicki was in shock, and was assuming this all was true. So why let a good thing stop, I thought. Keep going. She asked about the food and I said the food was fine, as far as college food goes, but the seating arrangements were terrible. The men and the women had to sit on either side of the dinning room and never got to sit together. She was looking a little pale, but I assured her that this wasn't all so bad. You still could wave to the other side and you could make it somewhat of a game to try to communicate across the room.

I was trying my best to keep a straight face. For me it was hard to do all this without smiling, because, after all, I was lying and painting a picture of Moody I had never seen. I rarely studied before 10:30 at night and my roommate I had were often told to turn our stereo down because it was knocking things off our neighbor's walls. The dining room was indeed a social gathering place and we could sit wherever we wanted. Often we found ourselves right by the back door to see all the new freshmen girls.

Vicki was so innocent and sweet, she actually thought she could handle all these rules, although it was a little more restrictive that she had anticipated. It was difficult to keep the facade up. I didn't want her to change her mind about Moody and I hoped that eventually she would know that I was just joking. However, she could walk out of the room and out of my life at any minute. I did not want to leave a bad impression the very first time we met, so I was going to tell the truth.

But then she asked me one more question and I couldn't resist lying again. "What was the social life like at Moody?"

I said the dating life at Moody was somewhat limited due to the fact that everyone studied so much. There was one phone on each floor, but you could only use it for five minutes at a time in order to allow other students the opportunity to use it. I was really going now, but Vicki was still excited about going to Moody and she was willing to work within the rules. So I continued.

I mentioned that you could date if they had a chaperone that accompanied you on the date. This was going a bit too far, but then Ken jumped in with a smirk on his face and said that he didn't ever recall me taking a chaperone with me on my many dates. He made it sound like I was this big dating machine, so I quickly changed the subject. Ken, however, jumped right back to the dating topic and again how often students date at Moody, implying that I was one who dated often. He even brought out how easy it was to date, especially when you, obviously referring to me, came to school with your already established relationship. Of course, he was talking about my former girlfriend, but he didn't know that we had just broken up. This was not ending up well. I was now wishing I had shared honestly with him what I was going through on the way down, but these lessons seem to come to me the hard way, and at the wrong time in my opinion. Well, I was learning my lesson well now.

Since I had come to a dead end in this topic, and I thought for sure that Vicki had noticed the awkwardness on my part about the dating scene, I smiled and confessed my sin of lying and hoped that Vicki wasn't upset. She was great and just laughed and said she was relieved that I was "stretching" the truth. I was relieved that she took it so well and we continued to talk for a few minutes about what Moody was really like. Then, they all excused themselves so they could get ready for a concert they were doing later on in the day.

Towards the end of Jim's stories, he got this real cute smirk on his face and said he needed to let me know that he had made up all the stories he told us about Moody. Oh brother, was I embarrassed. He must of thought that I was really immature and dumb to believe all these silly rules. What a dummy I was...so naive as usual. I turned red and just wanted to get out of there as soon as possible, but he was so gracious and said he was jut teasing and he had a great time. I shouldn't feel bad and he was glad I was going to Moody. Right, what was he really thinking? Here's this gullible, ditsy senior in high school. I figured he wasn't allowed to talk about his personal life or he thought it would be inappropriate, but it was obvious he had a girlfriend. Every time he mentioned something about dating, Ken, the assistant director of the public relations office would say something about it being nice when you bring your girlfriend to Moody. Jim, however, would act as if Ken hadn't mentioned anything at all. Strange, but he didn't have to share that part of his life if he didn't want to. I knew he must have a girlfriend though, because he was so nice and handsome. Oh well, so much for first impressions, we had to go to the auditorium to sing, and my cheeks hurt!

I was love struck and drifted through the rest of our time in the display area, hoping that I might somehow see this energetic girl again. Our schedule for the day brought us to the main auditorium, which would featureVicki's singing group. The meeting was basically pretty boring, but when the her group began to sing, it at least woke me up. The group itself was fair, but what really woke me up was watching Vicki. In my expert judgment, Vicki was the best thing they had going for them. I really couldn't take my eyes off of her. I hoped to see her again, but with my past with girls, I seriously doubted that I could get enough nerve to approach Vicki on my own. I was somewhat shy, and at times, very unsure about myself.

How shy was I? Listen to this story. When I was a sophomore in high school, there was this pretty girl, with medium blond hair, that sat in my basic algebra class. Our relationship consisted of looking at each other and perhaps, if it was my lucky day, we would say hi to each other. All year long, I never really took time to strike up a conversation, even though we were in the same class and even though I really wanted to say something to her. I was too shy.

Well, summer came and the opportunity had gone, or so I thought. My family always went camping during summer vacation for two or three weeks and this particular summer, we went to Colorado.

We were checking out of a campground named Whispering Pines, near the Royal Gorge, when something happened that I never dreamed would happen. We had broken camp and my dad was checking out of the campground, so my family and I were goofing around in the parking lot waiting for my dad to come out of the office. My brother and I were playing "throw stones at the tree," or something silly like that, when

I noticed that there was a girl standing by the car and trailer next to us that looked awfully similar to my dream girl in my algebra class back in Illinois. Well, instead of going up to this girl, who happened to look at me, and ask her, I pretended that I didn't see her and went around her car so I could see her license plate. This way I could just say that she looked like this girl from my school over one thousand miles away and not have to worry about talking to her. I looked at the car license plate, and to my unbelieving eyes, not only did it say Illinois, but the car dealership was from my home town. She really could be this girl from my school. What an opportunity. What a conversational piece that I could use for the next five years. She was still by her car. She occasionally looked at me, probably thinking the same thing about me. I took a deep breath and said to myself, forget it, she's probably not from your school and you would make yourself look ridiculous. So I did nothing. Can you believe it!

I'm not done. When my junior year of high school began, I walked into my geometry class, and there was that same girl. She was in my class again. She looked at me but only for a second, and then I went to find my seat. I never talked to her but the suspense was killing me. One of my friends, a girl, knew this other girl fairly well so I asked her if she knew where my dream girl went on vacation last summer. She said, "Colorado!" What an opening for a conversation now. I was sure I saw her. I could be confident. I could finally meet her! I never did. I never talked to her at all. To this day I don't know her name.

Well, here was another fine opportunity, and I wasn't sure if I would blow this one or not. After the concert, I "chickened out" again. I didn't tell Vicki how great she made the group look and sound. I didn't go up to her at all. Ken and I simply went back to pack up our display and head back to school.

After the program, I decided to run into the main hall to just say good-bye to Jim and Ken. They had been so nice and we had spent the whole afternoon with them. Even though I still felt dumb, I really had a great time and wanted to thank them for the info, so I ran, well walked quickly, into the hall and there they were, putting away all their supplies they had brought with them. What could I say?

"Oh hi, I just wanted to thank you for this afternoon. It was so fun. Of course, I'm pretty gullible, but it was great meeting someone from Moody. Maybe I'll see you again sometime."

Then Jim said, "Yeah, here's a business card."

I took it and turned it over.

"Now what's your name/" (DUMB question, as if I didn't know it).

But patiently and sweetly he said in his outgoing friendly voice,

"Jim...Jim Smith, actually James D. Smith on my mailbox. You don't want to get me mixed up with the other Jim Smith at Moody."

I was thinking, "Are you kidding, I could NEVER get you mixed up with another Jim Smith", but I wrote down James D. Smith anyway, acting cool but my heart beating out of my chest.

As we were packing up, I heard this familiar voice talking behind me. It was Vicki! I couldn't figure out why she was in this part of the church. She was with her friends again and when she came up to me, she had this beautiful smile and said that she wanted to write my name down so that she could say she knew someone at Moody.

I was thrilled that she came back to find me and that she wanted my name. My heart was pounding and I was starting to become very infatuated with this girl. I gave her my name and very professionally told her that it was a pleasure meeting her and that she had brightened up my day. Little did she know how bright she really had made my day!

James D. Smith, little did I know this would be one of the most important names to enter my life, ut I did know that this guy made a very positive impression on me... not that he would like me ,but just that God did have some other really neat Christian guys out there. So just wait! Now looking back, isn't it neat that one week after my break up and one night after Jim's break up, the Lord decided to have us meet for the very first time and it was a positive impression for both of us? We both needed to see HOPE in our futures!

"Be very careful, then, how you live, not as unwise but as wise. Make the most of every opportunity, because the days are evil." Ephesians 5:15, 16

Procrastination is a bad habit. Sometimes we miss opportunities because we are afraid to take that step, make that call, do that chore, write that letter. Don't put off until tomorrow what you can do today. You may never have that opportunity again. If it honors the Lord, do it.

Chapter Three

Blind Date

I returned to Moody and life went on. I continued to work for the public relations office and kept on with my studies. Now I'm not the world's best student, but I would eventually finish this semester with the best grade point average of my entire time at Moody. Doing well in school doesn't come from meeting a girl, but it did get my mind off the past and focus in on the here and now. After that weekend in Peoria, I realized that there were other girls in this world and I started to develop my own sense of worth. Life was still full of struggles, but at least the sun was shining. On the way home from Peoria, I did finally tell Ken that I was a single man and he realized that he had made my encounter

Some people like to make plans. Plans are good and help make the most of the time we have. However, leave room for plans to go wrong. Give yourself a little extra time traveling, you may get lost, have a flat tire or get stuck in traffic. Be willing to make some corrections while you are in the middle of the process.

Here's what I mean……

with Vicki a little difficult. He promised to make it up to me somehow. He really did.

It was great meeting somebody like "Jim Smith," however, as the days went by and turned into weeks my hope was diminishing and it was very hard going to school every day. I had to face my ex-boyfriend flirting with one of my friends, even watching their friendship bloom, while I was all alone. I was probably filled with a little jealousy, even though I didn't want to admit that to myself. Yes, that first Valentine's Day after the big breakup was tough, no flowers, no card, no candy, no teddy bear, no nothing!!! And after that, Spring arrived with all the budding romances popping up at school and not a single bud towards me, my hope was just about gone.

I think my mom and dad must have realized that I was a little sad and needed to be encouraged towards my other goals, so they came up with this idea in early March. They asked me if I'd like to go and visit Moody Bible Institute for a weekend to see what it was really like, since I was planning on attending there in the fall. I think they realized this would help that hope return and set my sights on other goals than just what was happening "at the moment" in my high school life. So plans were made but then plans had to be changed. My dad found out that he couldn't take off of work the Friday we were going to leave so we couldn't go. I think when my parents saw my disappointment, they decided I needed to go, even if it was without them. My dad called the Public Relations Director (remember the guy who was with Jim?) Ken, and asked if he would meet my plane and take me to Moody for that day, find a place for me to stay with a student and help me have a good time for the weekend. No problem... the agenda was set. Ken had quite a plan.

Several months after our February trip to Peoria, Ken called me into his office and said he had a very important job for me to do, if I wanted the job. He asked me if I remembered the girl we met down in Peoria. Of course I remembered her, but I pretended to think for a while and then said I remembered. "Her name was Vicki wasn't it?" Ken told me that he had just gotten off the phone with Vicki's dad. Her dad was flying Vicki up to Chicago to check out Moody's campus since her mom and dad couldn't find a time when all their schedules made it possible for all of them to come. So, my boss was to meet Vicki at the airport, arrange for her to visit some classes, to have her spend the night in the girl's dorm and to see what student life at Moody was all about. He had acquired tickets to the home basketball game that Friday night and asked me if I would like to be Vicki's date for the evening, joining him and his fiancée. We would then go out for ice cream following the game and he would treat all of us! What a deal! I couldn't pass it up. I accepted the invitation! Thus, Ken had made it up to me.

On the way back to Moody from the airport, Ken, the public relations guy, started to tell me all that was planned. Classes, chapel, a tour of the school, staying with some girls in the dorm, and even a blind date...yes with a college man! Oh no, a blind date and then he said not to worry because he and his fiance would double date with us and the guy was really nice. He also informed me the Jim Smith, the guy I had met in Peoria would introduce me to the girl I would be staying with that night. Jim worked for public relations and would meet me after classes and walk me to Houghton Hall, the dorm I would be staying in.

I had a great time visiting classes, chapel and meeting new people. Now I was to meet Jim, a familiar face and maybe he knew who my blind date was. I had so many questions and I was getting pretty nervous. He walked in, looking good, with his flashing smile and beautiful dark eyes...he had a presence that would charm anyone. I wondered how he and his girlfriend were getting along...

Late Friday afternoon I met Vicki in the public relations office. We were introduced and yes, she had remembered me and, of course, I remembered her. I was to take Vicki to the girls dorm, where she would met her roommate for the evening and also inform her of her "blind date" she had that evening. Ken only told her that he had arranged a date for that evening to the basketball game. As we were walking to the dorm, making small talk about her classes and trip on the plane, she suddenly asked me if I knew who her blind date was for the evening. I told her I did, and that I knew him well.

She wanted to know all about him. What he was like and if I thought he was a good person for her to go out with that evening. I assured her that she would have an enjoyable evening with this guy and that he was probably the perfect person for her first time at Moody. I told her that this guy had told me to tell Vicki to meet her at a pillar in the lobby near the girl's dorm elevator at 7:30pm. I told her not to worry about the date, but to enjoy dinner with the other girls and look forward to the evening. I never told her I was her date, and at this point, I felt pretty confident that the evening would go well.

"Hi Vicki, ready to go?"
"Sure."
Then Jim proceeded to tell me about the girl I was going to be staying with. I didn't care about the girl, I needed to know about this college man I was going to go out with. My heart was in my mouth, but I had to get some information.
"I hate to interrupt you, but Ken said something about a blind date for me tonight. Did he mention that to you?"

"Oh yeah, he did mention something about that," Jim replied.

"Do you know who he is? Is he nice? Is he good looking? Is he fun to be with?" I started firing questions right and left.

Finally Jim said, "Oh yeah, I know him. He's a real great guy, one of the nicest guys her at the school, in fact, he told me to give you a message. You're supposed to meet him at the middle pillar in the lobby at 7:30. "Don't worry," were his last words to me, "you're going to have a great time!"

"Yeah, easy for you to say," I thought.

Eunice, the girl I stayed with in the dorm didn't know anything about my blind date, so I got ready as quickly as I could. I didn't want to be late and I didn't want to be over-dressed, but I wanted to look just like the other college girls, so I brushed out my hair, put on some jeans and a warm sweater (it was snowing in March) and a little lipstick and I was ready to go. Before I knew it, I was in the elevator, coming down from the tenth floor to the lobby to meet my Mr. College Man!

The doors opened, my knees were knocking as I looked at the pillar to see my blind date leaning casually against the pillar with the most mischievous grin ever, it was Jim. I thought I would die! He must really think I was stupid. What had I asked him about my blind date? Were they dumb questions? Would he be sorry he'd volunteered for this blind date stuff? Could these doors just close and then I could go back to the safety of the tenth floor?

Just about at that moment, Jim stood straight up and said, now with the most charming smile again, "Hi, come on or we'll be late to the basketball game!"

She looked somewhat embarrassed when she saw me leaning against the pillar and realized that I was her date for the evening. She laughed at how I again had lied to her. I clearly pointed out that I had not lied, but had only told the truth. I had just left some thing unsaid.. She agreed and we walked over to the basketball game. I was feeling pretty good. A date with Vicki, and Ken was buying everything afterwards. What could go wrong?

The game went well and we were enjoying our time together. We were to meet Ken at the office after the game. I was looking forward to this double date. I would be with Vicki, Ken was buying, and we would be driving out to the suburbs to a great ice cream shop. I didn't have a car, so getting out of the city every once in awhile was a treat.

As we made it to the office hallway, I looked for Ken. My good feeling started to fade away went I saw a enveloped taped to the office door with "Jim Smith" written in big bold letters. This couldn't be good. This could only mean Ken wasn't coming. Perhaps he was going to meet us at a different location. I slowly opened the letter and read it. My heart went cold. I stood there and just stared at the letter, looking like a statue. Ken was not coming, something had come up. I had no car, no double date, no ice cream shop in the suburbs and very little money.

And off we went. The basketball game was a lot of fun and afterwards, Jim said we were going to the public relations office to meet Ken and his fiancee to go out for ice cream at a great ice cream parlor. Sounded like fun and this guy was so much fun. Suddenly the hall we walked down to the office sure was quiet and Jim's steps seemed to get slower and slower. Up ahead on the office door, I saw a note taped to the door. I think Jim saw it first as he ripped in off and then continued to stare at it for a few minutes. Obviously something was wrong and I was almost too scared to ask what was wrong.

But then I finally decided to plunge right into his thoughts and asked, "What's wrong?"

Where was I going to go on this date now? What were we going to do? I stood there for what seemed like hours, until Vicki, who had read the letter over my shoulder said, "Oh well, too bad they can't come. I hope it isn't serious. We'll have fun. What do you what to do?" At this point in my life, I began what became a habit during my college days, thinking of an inexpensive, yet hopefully fun date. I didn't have much money, but I offered to take Vicki around the city and then out for come pizza. I could only buy a small pizza, but I figured this would be fine, since she didn't seem like a big eater, and Chicago style pizza is very thick. She loved the idea and we headed to the girls dorm so she could get into some warmer clothes to walk around the windy city. I liked this girl's attitude and my good feeling was back.

Jim finally replied, "Ken says something came up and he's sorry but they can't meet us?"

"Oh." I hoped it wasn't too bad. We still had the rest of the evening and all of Chicago to discover, but maybe Jim didn't want to spend the rest of the evening with me.

"Well, it's too bad they can't come," I was trying to sound optimistic, because Jim looked so sad. "So, what do you want to do?"

I waited for his answer. Here was his chance to get out of it.

"Do you want to see Chicago?"

Do I want to see Chicago? Do you want to take me? Have I always dreamed of walking around the city with a great looking college guy and the snow falling gently in the moonlight? Could he hear my heart beating?

"Sure, that would be fun," I answered as nonchalantly as I could.

Off we went into the big city that seemed softer with the snowflakes fluttering all around. Now I know I must sound like a hopeless romantic, but it was one of the most wonderful nights of my life. The tall buildings with all the lights, the music of the traffic, the crispness in the air, the newness of a big city, the independence of going wherever I chose, the night sky, and the protection of an older man who knew all the ropes all intertwined to weave together that enchanting evening. It was a dream that I never wanted to end. Just at that moment as I looked into that starry night, I got a wonderful idea. There in the front of us stood the John Hancock building, one of the tallest buildings in Chicago.

As we walked around Chicago, I managed to save Vicki's life on several occasions. I'm not sure if she was not used to seeing so many tall buildings or that the traffic in her small mid-western town did not have the crazy taxi drivers like Chicago did, but she would often walk right into the street, gazing at the beautiful buildings shining into the night sky, oblivious to the night traffic or the red traffic lights. I would grab her arm and pull her back to the safety of the sidewalk, just as a car would go flying in front of us, reminding her that these drivers will not stop for her while she was busy sightseeing. In the process of saving her life, I unexpectedly accomplished two ever rewarding things. First, I got to touch Vicki's arm. Now, I know it wasn't for a very long time, but the tingling feeling was there. The other accomplishment was that by constantly pulling Vicki out of the path of rushing traffic, I managed to get Vicki to stay close to me while she looked at the sights. This was an arrangement that I could handle.

When we came to the John Hancock building, one to the tallest buildings in the world, Vicki asked if we could go up to the top and see the lights of the city. I had been to the top before and the view was spectacular, but it also cost some money, and I had just enough for a small pizza. That's all. Going to the top would cost more than a small pizza, so I started to make excuses about why we shouldn't go up to the top. Believe it or not, I actually told Vicki that the night wasn't clear enough to get a good view. What a liar. Now understand that Vicki had been gazing up into the night sky for the last half hour. She knew the sky had cleared and was now crystal clear! After a few minutes more attempts at lying, she looked at me and said, "you don't have enough money, do you?" I liked the honesty in this girl. Vicki was always honest and to the point. I was always trying to impress her with what I thought she would like in me. I decided that if there was going to be anything between us, I would just be me, and she would have to like me for who I was.

I honestly said back to her, "No, I only have enough money for a small pizza."

She said, "Fine, let's go get some pizza!" That was it, no big deal. So we went and ordered a small pizza.

"How about going up the John Hancock building and looking over the entire city?" I suggested, proud of a great idea.

"Oh, no, we don't want to do that. We wouldn't see anything tonight," replied Jim.

Now as I looked up into the sky, I realized it was one of the most clear, crisp evenings, the kind of night where you could see every star so clearly that one wanted to reach out to touch them.

So of course I encouraged him, "It's one of the clearest nights ever, Jim."

"Well," he continued, "There's probably a real long line and it will take too long before we can go up the elevator."

I glanced over to where the line was to be formed, and there wasn't a single person in line.

"No, look Jim, there's no line. Aren't we lucky?"

I wasn't quite sure what was wrong, but I was beginning to realize that he didn't WANT to go up the John Hancock, at least with me. He stood there contemplating his next reason and that made me realize what was wrong. He didn't have enough money. That must be it, because I knew we were having a good time. Poor Jim. I didn't care if he didn't have enough money, he just needed to tell me. I'd help him by showing him it didn't matter to me about the money, but that "honesty" DID matter. He just had to tell me the truth.

"Jim, you don't have enough money do you?"

"No, well not enough to go up to the John Hancock observation deck AND have a small pizza."

"Why didn't you just tell me? Let's just go for the small pizza!"

And we did. After ordering, we sat and talked and talked. Honesty had opened the doors. It had been about a month since both of us had been "dumped" and really neither one of us had talked about it much to anyone. Anyone who had been "dumped" knows there are many feelings to work through and questions asked and things one learns about oneself. This was a wonderful moment where two people who had gone through the same experience got the chance to talk through all these issues. We both felt safe in sharing our feelings and actually as we helped one another, we were helping ourselves. I was so impressed with Jim's honesty and kindness and politeness. This man had impeccable manners and treated me like a lady. He was definitely a remarkable person and a great conversationalist. A song kept playing on the jukebox that night that seemed to mirror our feelings even though neither one of us realized it at the time. The words to the chorus of this song were,

> *"My eyes adored you,*
> *like a million miles away from me*
> *you couldn't see my eyes adored you...*
> *So close, so close and yet so far.."*

We also carved our names into the booth of the Pizza Inn, it was a tradition there for a couple to do this, however, we carved out our names separately in separate places, to be seen again at another time.

While we ate, we talked. Not just the little things, but we shared with each other our lives. We opened the doors of our hearts, just enough to show what we were really made of. We were honest. We were real. We found out that each of us had been "dumped" in our relationships just before we met at the college fair. We opened up and just shared with each other what we felt like and how it had happened and the way we made it through. We talked about fun things, family, futures, friends, summers and school. It was a time for each of us to get to know the other person in a simple way. No romantic, long term relationship was made at that table that night, but an honest friendship between two people started to grow. A seed in the right place, at the right time was planted. As we talked, a song played in the background that I will always remember. Neither of us said anything about the song that night, but we both remembered it. "My Eyes Adored You." Before we left, we carved our names into the booth. Maybe because of "The Waltons" old TV show or because I was just being silly, instead of carving "Jim" in the booth, I scratched the name "Jim Bob". I would later regret that carving.

It was time to return to Moody, so once again we were walking through the "winter wonderland," however, we were walking back a much quieter way. I sure was glad that this Jim knew his way around the city. All of a sudden a bag lady started coming right towards me, asking if I had any money. She wasn't looking a t Jim, but straight at me and getting closer and closer. Being from a small town, I had never been approached in this way, and to be honest I was very fright-ened, so I pulled Jim right in front of me to be between us, the

*lady and me. He very gently but sternly said we had nothing
to give her (which was the absolute truth!) And she needed to
keep on going. Then he took my arm and we walked around
her and on our way. He had taken such great control and in a
sense been my"knight in shining armor". However, now this
city didn't look like a winter wonderland anymore. It was full
of strangers and danger and I wanted to feel safe, so I asked
Jim if I could hold his arm on the way home. He was so sweet.
He just smiled and held out his arm as he replied, "Sure."*

As we walked back to Moody, we passed by a bag lady
who asked Vicki for some money. Vicki grabbed by arm and
hid behind me as I told the lady that we didn't have anything
to give to her. I felt bad about having this happen to Vicki,
but it turned out to be another highlight of the evening. After
we had walked around the corner, a somewhat shaken, but
brave little country girl asked me if she could hold onto
my arm while we walked back to school. I smiled and said
"Sure." Inside I shouted, "I can't believe it! This is unbeliev-
able!" As we walked back to Moody I wondered if anyone
would see us. I didn't have to wonder long though. A block
away from Moody, Vicki felt safe and let go of my arm. We
said good night as I dropped her off at her dorm and drifted
off to my room.

*I grabbed his arm tightly but not too close for I didn't
want him to feel awkward or like I was after him or anything.
I just wanted to feel safe and his strong arm definitely gave
me protection. He was such a gentleman and didn't make me,
a little senior in High School from the country, feel stupid.
He took me safely to the lobby of Houghton Hall and we said
good bye. He even offered to meet me for breakfast the next
morning before my bus left. "This guy was really great at
this job," I thought.*

We had made arrangements for me to meet her for breakfast and then for me to escort her to the bus stop that would take her back to the airport. My roommate knew something strange was happening, because I NEVER got up for breakfast on a Saturday morning. Just before the bus left for the airport, I gave my Moody address to Vicki. I had complained that this poor college student never got any mail, and I would love to get some friendly mail. She promised to write if I would write first. I promised. I also asked for her phone number, but she wouldn't give me that either. I was determined that I would find her address and phone number somehow. I did work in the public relations department. We said good-bye and off she went. Would we ever see each other again? I didn't know. Would we write often? I hoped so. All I knew so far was that I had a great weekend and really liked spending time with Vicki.

After our breakfast the next morning, Jim picked up my suitcase and walked the six blocks to the hotel, where the airport bus was to pick me up. We had some extra time so we sat down in the hotel lobby to talk. Jim had been saying that since his family lived in a suburb and saw him every Sunday at Moody Church, (his father was an assistant pastor there at the time) he never really received any mail in his P.O. Box and I said, "I'll write you to fill up that box." So he had written his address and phone number on an index card and gave it to me at this time. I smiled, but as we talked I remembered that I had decided to not write or call a boy first, so just before I got up on the bus, I thanked him for the evening and the breakfast and then ripped up his card and gave it back to him. With a smile, I replied, "I really don't write guys first!" As I sat down in the bus seat and waved to him, my mind was racing. "What if he thought that was dumb or immature. How will he be able to write me now? He doesn't even have my address. Well, I guess I'll just have to see what happens but no matter what I've had a wonderful weekend and met a new friend." As the plane took off and I could see all of the Chicago area, I didn't realize what a special friend I had made but I knew he was an amazing guy and I would never forget this weekend. Next year, watch out Moody, here I come!

I sent Vicki a letter within a couple days and she wrote back. Then I sent her a birthday card and later wrote her a letter that could have been taken romantically or just friendly. I also included her phone number that I had found. I waited to see how she would respond. I never received a letter from her after that letter. Oh well, no harm done, but it looked like there would be no budding romance either. Summer was coming anyway, and distant relationships don't do well, especially during the summer. Only God knew what summer would bring.

A girl needs to give up control in her relationships. No conniving, no games, no pretending. Just be honest and ask him honest questions and GIVE UP the control. Enjoy his leadership, let him lead where you go, what you do and yet be honest with him and be honest with yourself. Give him the opportunity to lead, instead of taking it from him and not giving him a chance to take on the leadership. You will see a more clearer and honest "picture" of who he really is as you watch him lead in your friendship. After all, you need to honestly ask yourself if this is someone you can and want to follow and submit to for your life. Is he a good leader for you? Also remember to give him room to grow in his leadership because a young man is just learning to lead early in his life. Is he maturing and growing in his leadership?

It is the unexpected things in our life that
often turns out to be the most memorable events
in our lives. The car accident you never planned on,
an illness in the family, an unscheduled counseling
time with a friend or a complete stranger or a friend
not showing up for a scheduled double date.
God allows these events in our lives to strengthen
us to become more like Jesus Christ. He never
wastes an experience. We need to be people that
are willing to be inconvenienced. A disappointment or unscheduled appointment may just be HIS
APPOINTMENT !! God may just be bringing
someone into your life for a very important meeting.

*And we know that God causes everything to work
together for the good of those who love God and
are called according to his purpose for them.*
Romans 8:28 (NLT)

Chapter Four

Summer Alone

⚜

I really just wanted to have a relationship. I thought I needed to have a girlfriend, but what I really needed was to fall in love with myself. To enjoy the type of person that God made me to be. To stop comparing myself to others or try to be the person I thought people would want to be with. I needed to become confident in myself and my Lord. Confidence in who you are is one of the best ways to become attractive to others.

And I really needed to be completely obedient to the Lord in choosing to be submissive to my parents, "because this is right". (Not because it makes sense to me or it is easy for me. Submission happens when it takes personal sacrifice and choice to place yourself under someone else. That is why the perfect place to learn "submission" is under you parents, especially as you grow older as a teenager and early adulthood. You feel more independent but you choose to submit to your parent's rules or ways.)

This summer would prove to be a training ground for a lifelong lesson in submission, which a wife is also commanded to do so let the training begin!

Here's what we mean…..

The summer turned out to be a pivotal point in my life. It was during that summer that I learned to be myself. Often I had tried to be the person that I thought would be liked by most people. If I thought I would be accepted by more people I knew if I was funny, I tried to be funny. Sometimes I was funny, but there always was someone else who came along and was funnier. At times, I thought being an athlete was the way to go, and to know the scores of all the professional teams was important. So I did that too and someone else came along that was better.

I tried many things and there was ALWAYS someone better.

This went over into my dating relationships. If a girl wanted me to be intellectual, I tried to act that way. If she thought all movies were wrong to go see, then I thought that way also. If she wanted a romantic, I was Mr. Romance. Not all these things are bad. Romance, sports, academics and humor are all good, but at times they are not me. There are times a person should try to improve on his social and interpersonal relationship skills, but we should always be the person we are, the person God created us to be.

I once heard a saying that I never forgot. "To try to be like someone else is to waste the person you are." That summer I followed that advice. I accepted myself for who I was and learned to live with my talent, abilities, and personality. I learned that there are some things I'll never be, and I started to accept that fact. I understood what I could change in me and prayed for God's help to do it, and started to grow in wisdom so I would know the difference.

Friends Forever

So the summer was not to be a great summer of romance. I was the director of the counselor training program at my church's camp. That was my official title. Unofficially, I was the counselor getting the training. I literally had a great summer. I made several friends, enjoyed being with many people and learned a great deal about responsibility. This summer made me content with who I was. With all that happened that summer, the most memorable part of the entire summer was that God taught me to be myself. The training was done, the tests were about to begin.

My summer was also to be a "training program." I was very busy working all summer to get money for Moody Bible Institute, but I also wanted to just have fun. I met a great Christian guy and we started liking each other...what's wrong with that? The only thing wrong was that my parents didn't want me to date him.

Of course, being the mature "grown up" high school graduate that I was, I didn't believe my parents had any good reason to ask me not to see him. Actually it was much more difficult than that. I would have many discussions with my parents about what a great guy he was an how he treated me well, how others were impressed with him, and how he loved the Lord. My parents even KNEW his parents, so what was their problem? Their reply was that they really didn't have a good reason for me not to date him, they thought he was a great guy too. They just felt that I shouldn't be dating him and they had to ask me not to date him, because they felt that that was right. They were going to have to answer to the Lord and they had to be honest with me about how they felt. Instead of just trusting them and obeying them, I tried to sneak behind their backs to see this guy and then deal with my guilt (or pretend the guilt really wasn't there!)

However, God wants complete obedience, not just obedience when it makes sense to us. Children are given the

49

*command to honor and obey their parents, for this is RIGHT!
I needed to learn about complete submission to my parents.
Submission does not happen when both parties agree, but
submission comes at a point when there are two opposing
views an one has to "submit" or willingly place themselves
under someone else. The reason it was an important lesson
I needed to learn this summer was that you are not totally
right in your relationship with God if you are knowingly
sinning in a certain area. I would practically deceive myself
by having devotions each day and thinking that my relationship with God was fine. Just having devotions does not make
your relationship with God right; you must OBEY what you
know is RIGHT ! Therefore, I finally realized by the end of
the summer that I needed to completely obey and submit
to my parent's request of not seeing, talking or writing this
young man, no matter what I thought or felt.*

*Even though it was one of the toughest phone calls I had
to make by obeying what my parents had asked me to do
(with their permission), it brought me more peace than I
had had in a long time, at least all summer. At last I was
doing exactly what God wanted. Even though they never
gave me a reason and it seemed such an extreme command,
and one that I didn't agree with or understand, I realized
that submission and doing it God's way was RIGHT and the
BEST! These were great lessons to learn and further tests
in this submission and following God COMPLETELY were
about to begin!*

I never looked forward to school, but coming back to
Moody as a second year student was a lot more enjoyable
than as a freshman. You knew the ropes. You had a sense of
confidence because you could see all the freshmen walking
around like you did just a year ago. This year was going to
be different. Little did I know how different. It would change
my life!

We need to remember to put God first in all things.
We are on earth to glorify him. If we understand
that, then we will get through life much easier.
God is not here to make our lives more comfortable,
God is here to help us become more like Christ.
When we finally make God more important than
anything else in our lives, then he will give us
blessings. Put God first, before your money,
your recognition and your relationships.

*"But seek first his kingdom and his righteousness,
and all these things will be given to you as well."
Matthew 6:33 NIV*

Chapter Five

The Leach

⸎

We never know who is watching us. At times we think the whole world is watching, especially when we fail, but then we learn that not many people really care about what WE are doing, because they are only interested in what THEY are doing. However, there are those other times when we don't think anyone is watching and they really ARE watching and listening. So basically, we should live our lives as if someone is always watching us. Here is one of my embarrassing moments...

Vicki was a faint memory of the previous semester. All summer went by and we didn't communicate, and I wasn't sure what would happen between us. I didn't even know if Vicki would remember me. When I arrived I did see her walking around the campus, but I never took the time to go up to say hi. Besides, she was usually surrounded by other people, and mostly other interested guys, as far as I was concerned.

One of the brave things I did new this year was join the Men's Choir. All last year some of my friends were encouraging me to join, but I never thought I could sing that well to be in the group. They assured me that it didn't take a major in music to sing. All I needed, they said, was the ability to follow the director and stay on the same note as everyone else.

I finally got enough nerve to try out. I was amazed that I actually made it. I think the director wanted to show students that it wasn't so hard to make Men's Choir. It turned out to be a real enjoyable time. I made new friends. We toured the USA singing in all parts of the country, and I learned to accept new responsibilities, like fitting in three practices each week to my already busy schedule. I found out that with a little more discipline, this new addition to my schedule was no problem. It actually made me a more disciplined person. It also made me a more sociable person.

I often wanted to be a little more sociable with Vicki, but I never got up the nerve to go up to her. There was that problem of her always seemingly having people around her. I didn't want to embarrass myself or her by going up to her and asking if she remembered me. I thought that would be really dumb.

There was this other problem also. It seemed that Vicki had become acquainted with someone rather quickly and they would often be sitting together in the dinning room or talking together in the plaza. This was fine to most people, but it really bothered me. Here she was already with some guy, and I never even got a chance to say hi. In fact I thought that this guy was not Vicki's type, but I guess I had the wrong idea of who Vicki was. So, I got angry every time I saw them together.

However, with Vicki out with this new guy, it made me feel less guilty about what I did with the Men's Choir every Tuesday and Thursday. This sounds really bad, but it's true. Each week, after our afternoon practices, most of the club would go directly to the dining hall for dinner. We would then all sit at the tables closest to the conveyor belt, so we could check out all the new freshmen girls! We would rate them on a scale of one to ten.

One particular evening, just after practice, Vicki happened to be in the dining room and walked right in front of all of us. She rated high in many judge's opinions, but in my opinion, and I let everyone know it, she was a twenty five. I especially liked her legs! Now with a score that high, everyone was curious as to why I was not dating this girl! I didn't have time to tell them the whole story, so I simply said that she was a leech! I suddenly got kicked in the leg!

I wasn't sure why I got kicked until I turned around to see Vicki. She had seen me and actually had remembered me. I supposed that she had come over to say hi. What a dummy I felt like. Everyone at the table started to laugh and I turned beet red. I said hi, great to see you and she returned the favor, but I'm sure she felt like a fish out of water. Here were a bunch of upperclassmen laughing their heads off at this freshman girl saying hi to a "long lost friend." She made a quick, but gracious exit, and I felt like a total idiot!

I loved everything about Moody. I loved studying the Bible, living in the dorm with the other girls, making friends and having a whole bunch of Christian young men as potentials. All through high school, there were nice boys but not Christians, so I didn't want to date them. Now most (hopefully all) the guys at Moody were Christians so the choices increased.

During Freshman Orientation week, there were many activities to get to know one another before all the upperclassmen joined the freshmen at Moody, so I did make many new friends. I went out on a few dates and enjoyed some and really didn't like others. I remembered the evening that I had had with Jim Smith six months earlier. I remembered that he had been so much fun and so polite. I would look for him at different times, but never saw him. Oh well, I was meeting many other people.

There was one upperclassman who was especially nice to me and asked me out on three to four dates... almost every night of this one week...these weren't just "little inexpensive" dates that many Moody men had to do because they were paying their school bills and didn't have a lot of fun money, but this guy took me to nice restaurants, and ended the week with a cruise down the Chicago River where he kept getting closer and closer to me, which made me feel very uncomfortable. I really felt like I didn't know him very well. I had only dated him one week and we really were just beginning our acquaintance.

The next day we went to church together, ate lunch and then went to the Lincoln Park Zoo where this young man proceeded to tell me that we couldn't date anymore because he didn't think that I would make a good missionary's wife. This statement upset me for two reasons. First of all, he didn't really know me after one week of dating to make that kind of statement and then I took that statement as the ultimate insult because I wanted to be in full time Christian work, perhaps missions, so I was very offended.

I let him know that I was very offended and how dare he decide whether or not I would make a good missionary's wife, especially since he didn't really know me to make that kind of decision. God could use whomever He wanted to. This young man was right about one thing though: there would be no more dates for us. After me, this guy would date a different girl (even two of my good friends on my dorm floor) each week and dump them in the same way!

Well on the Tuesday after the famous "zoo" day, I was taking my tray back to the conveyer belt after eating in the cafeteria. I looked over and for the first time since I began Moody, I saw Jim Smith. I mentioned it to my friend and decided to go over and say, "hi." I thought it would be fun to surprise him so I went behind him and said, "Hi Jim, do you remember me?" He turned bright red all the way to his

*ears. He said hello but seemed very uneasy and uncomfort-
able with me being there so I quickly said, "Nice to see you
again. Thought I'd just say hi, but I have to go now!"*

*As I walked out of the cafeteria doors with my friend,
I heard Jim's whole table howl in laughter. I felt so stupid.
Why did I have to go and say hi to him? Here I was a lowly
freshman coming up to an upper classman in front of all his
"cool" friends and I had totally embarrassed him. I'd never
do that again to Jim! He had taken me out as part of his job
and he was probably glad he was done. That's probably why
I hadn't seen him, up to now, at Moody. He stayed away from
where I was so as not to be embarrassed. I wouldn't make
this mistake again. My heart felt very sad and embarrassed
but it was over and now I knew where I stood. How wrong
could one be!*

I should have gone after Vicki and explained the situation to her, but I just let it go. Perhaps she really didn't feel
bad. Maybe I'll see her later. At least the ice was broken. We
had made contact, and although it was rough, it was a start.

So, no matter where I am, I have learned to speak
truthfully and be encouraging with my words.
You never know who may be listening.

"Encourage one another and build each other up"
1 Thessalonians 5:11 NIV

Chapter Six

Pursuit of A Dream

～～

Sitting around waiting for something to happen is sometimes valuable, but there are also times when you have to take some initiative and take the first step. . If there is something you can do, a call to make, a place to be, or words to say, then "Do it", "Go for it", "Don't just sit there, do something" are all phrases that come to my mind. A relationship doesn't just happen. It takes work to help it to develop. Trying to build our relationship took some time and action!

There is a good hint for girls to remember as they begin an interest in someone. Let the guy lead. If a guy really likes you or is interested in you, he will work to get you. You don't have to make things happen or wonder if he likes you. He will go after you and you will KNOW he is interested. He is made a man, wanting to conquer, so just be you and be honest. A relationship takes work, but let the guy lead. Don't manipulate or connive, just follow and enjoy his pursuit of you. If it is not meant to be, you'll live. Here's Jim's pursuit of me….

After our initial meeting in the dining room, I knew that I had to make our next meeting more positive. I soon found a way to perhaps mend the broken bridge.

My boss once again asked me to go down to Peoria for another college fair at Grace Presbyterian Church. I would be the person representing Moody this time, since Ken would not be accompanying me. He told me that I could take another guy with me if I wanted the company. I thought of a friend from Men's Choir named Rick, who might want to join me for a long Saturday of travel. I asked Rick and he said yes. We were ready to go.

I did remember that Vicki lived down near Peoria, so I thought I would ask her if she wanted a free ride down to her home. Great idea, so I waited where I knew I would see her, in the dining room, by the tray return.

Sure enough, after waiting for a while with my tray, there she came. Of course I had to be casual about it, pretending that I just happened to be returning my tray at the identical moment that she was, and I caught her eye. I said, "Hi!" Now I had to do the hard part, carry on an intelligible conversation with some very attractive girl I wanted to impress. This was almost like asking her for a date. We were by the exit, and time was running out. So I just did it, I started talking.

She thought the idea was great, but....(I hate that word) BUT she was already going down to her home that weekend to play the organ for a wedding. I found out that she played the organ, BUT she had to be home for the Friday night rehearsal, BUT thanks for thinking of her. That was a partial victory, BUT it wasn't what I had planned..

Wow, was I surprised the next Thursday when Jim Smith was putting his cafeteria tray on the conveyer belt right by me and said a very friendly "Hi, how are you doing?" He was very handsome, had sparkling brown eyes and a wonderful smile. He didn't seem embarrassed at all.

In fact, this time we walked out the cafeteria doors TOGETHER! He actually seemed interested in talking to me. Then he came up with this idea out of nowhere. He was going to be the representative for Moody in Peoria at the same college fair we had met each other at six months ago! He thought maybe I'd like to ride along with him and his friend and visit home for one day. That was so nice of him - probably once again for his job- but it would be great fun- however, I was playing the organ for one of my close friend's wedding that weekend and was actually going home on the train on Friday, but it was nice of him to ask me.

Rick and I took off a little late that Saturday, but as we got closer to Peoria, the conversation turned to Vicki. Rick knew that I had met some girl here last year, and he asked if I knew where she lived. He said we might get a meal out of the visit and any home cooked meal is worth the effort. I knew she lived in Morton, so we pulled off the expressway and headed for the nearest public phone. I also knew her last name was Sutter, but when we looked in the phone book, we saw many "Sutter's". Time was limited and we didn't want to call every one of them. We didn't have much change either.

I looked at the addresses. I wrote to Vicki a few times but I didn't remember her address. I had one guess. Rick called. I was scared. Her mom answered. Good guess. Rick explained that we were friends of Vicki and we were in the area and wondered if we could come over to say "Hi" before we went to the college fair.

We arrived at her home and her mom walked us over to the church where Vicki was indeed practicing the organ. She was in the lobby and when she saw us she came running toward us. She was ready for the wedding and had this beautiful brown and gold dress on. She looked like an angel. For a second I thought she was going to jump into my arms, but she stopped short and welcomed us to her church. We didn't have much time to talk, and she had to get ready for the eleven o'clock wedding, so we said goodbye and started to leave.

It was then that Rick's dream came true. Vicki's mom asked if we had time to stop back for dinner. We had time. Rick got his meal.

Friday's rehearsal went well but I still went over to practice early on Saturday morning, so I had my long dress on and practiced with my curlers in my hair, so as to accomplish two feats at the same time. All of a sudden someone came running into the sanctuary screaming, "Emergency phone call from your mom - hurry up!" My heart pounded as I ran for the phone. She called to say two friends of mine had come over there to our house and she would bring them to the church so they should be there any minute! Their names were Jim and Rick. It registered in my head of Jim's offer of bringing me home for the day and my heart pounded as I realized he still came to see me. However, I couldn't think of anyone I knew named Rick. Anyway, there I was, standing in a long gown with curlers in my hair. Seeing that our home was only three houses away from our church, I dashed to the women's bathroom, ripped out my curlers, brushed through my hair, put on some lip gloss and perfume and came out in time to see Jim and his friend and my mom standing in our church foyer. Jim was looking very good once again, dressed in order to make a great impression to future students of Moody. I ran to greet them and they were very funny and friendly, but I realized I needed to start playing the prelude for the wedding and guests would soon start coming so as I excused myself, my mom invited them to come later on that evening for supper and Rick was quick to say yes. College guys are always up for a good home-cooked meal! So, I'd see them again in a few hours. I couldn't believe it. That meant my schedule was pretty packed - a wedding, a recep-

tion, dinner with these two Moody "friends" and then a date coming to take me to a concert at my church later on that evening.

We came back after an afternoon at the college fair, which was not as exciting as the year before. When we arrived at the house, Vicki's mom greeted us at the door and then introduced us to her husband, Vicki's father. Fathers can be pretty intimidating, and although Vicki's dad was tall, he was very friendly and in his own way, gentle. He invited us into the family room, where some football game was on. This was good, since I enjoyed football, and perhaps could relate with Vicki's dad. Dads are important in a girl's life and I didn't want her dad not to like me.

We sat down to watch the game and talk. After a few minutes, Vicki came out in some jeans and a blue striped sweater. From then on I had always liked that sweater on Vicki, until she washed it in hot water one day and gave it to her little three year old sister. This does show that first impressions are important, if not always true, they do make a lasting impression. We made some small talk, but Rick proved to be the better conversationalist, so I did the old "fake like you're sleeping" trick. By doing this, I didn't have to talk, but I could still hear what people were saying.

Couples do this often while they are dating. The reason is a little different, but it still eliminates the need to talk. Couples can fake like they are sleeping, and then put their heads on one another's shoulder. They can be close without the need to open their souls. It works for a short time, but sooner or later, to get closer in a relationship, you have to talk.

As soon as I realized that Rick was benefiting from my sleeping episode, I "woke up". It was too late and it was time to eat. We had fun though and it was nice to be in Vicki's home and meet her parents. I did find out that I already had a good reputation with Vicki's folks because I was the one who escorted her around Moody the year before and they were thankful that I had helped her out. That compliment made me feel good.

We went back to the college fair and finished up the evening. On the way back we thought we should stop in one more time to say thank you. To our disappointment, no one was home, but we used some stones to spell "Thanks" on the sidewalk, and then we left for Moody

I ran home after the reception in order to get ready for my big night with three guys. As I was getting ready, I heard the knocks and heard Jim and Rick come in and start talking to my dad. They seemed to be enjoying themselves, so that gave me a few extra minutes. When I walked into the family room, they were watching football, but Jim commented on what a nice sweater I had on. "Wow, he noticed!" I thought, "Oh I'd better wear this sweater more often."

Rick, Jim and I continued to talk until I realized that Jim fell asleep in our lazy boy arm chair. I figured he was tired since he had left early that morning to drive down here to Peoria for three hours, talked with kids at the college fair and now got to relax a minute. While Jim slept, Rick continued to talk to me. He seemed a little interested in me which was very flattering.

Jim woke up in time for our home- made spaghetti supper and we had lots of fun together during the supper time. Mom packed the leftovers for the boys, and they kept teasing that they were going to come back later on. I really hoped they would, but didn't know if they were serious or not. They left to go back to the college fair in Peoria and about a half an hour later my date came to pick me up for the concert. At the end of the concert, I was wondering if my "friends" would be returning, but the concert had gone long so I thought it was too late.

As my date was walking me to the door, I saw all these rocks on my sidewalk. What had happened - then I noticed that they spelled out the work "t-h-a-n-k-s" and I smiled. They HAD come back, but nobody had been home so they creatively thanked us for our hospitality and let us know they had returned! I informed my date that two Moody guys were in the area working and my mom had invited them over for supper. He probably wasn't too pleased, but I was very excited. Maybe they were a little interested in me - at least Rick was and Jim was really nice, fun, cute and liked his job or could he be INTERESTED too? Maybe. Whatever happened it sure had been a fun day and they were neat guys who were great fun!.

On the way back, Rick mentioned that he would like to date Vicki. I told him that I had the same idea, and since I knew her longer, he should back off for awhile. He said fine, but only for a little while. Good friends help one another. Rick was a good friend, because he gave me a reason to pursue Vicki in a little more obvious way. Time was running out.

I appreciated the words of my friend, but I also realized I needed to wake up and get going. His words and actions were something I needed to hear.

"As iron sharpens iron, a friend sharpens a friend."
Proverbs 27:17

Chapter 7

Making An Impression

≫

Making an impression is a funny kind of thing. Sometimes when you try really hard, it flops and you make an impression that you really didn't want to make. The harder you try to make an impression, the more you focus on yourself and what others think of you, rather than focusing on the person you're trying to get to know. Don't get me wrong, impressions are important, but they should be honest and real, if you want the relationship to last. They should reveal your true self and don't try to be someone you're not. Just be yourself, and hopefully you are the kind of person that will bring out the best in others as you allow God to develop the best in you.

Another good hint, when first forming a friendship or relationship is that your first impression of someone could be wrong. Just because of something said or done the first time you meet or go out with them, you may make your whole impression of what you think a person is like by what you create up in your mind. However, your "made up impression" could be so strong in your mind that you truly are blinded to the real person. Just remember you always want to make a good first impression but you could be wrong about your first impressions of someone else. Time and honesty are very valuable when establishing your foundation of a forever friendship. Here we are making and receiving our first impressions of one another...

I was very excited when Jim called me up on the phone a few days after the fun dinner at my house in Morton. He called just to say thank you again to my mom for the home-made dinner and we talked. I told him I liked the "thanks" sign on my sidewalk. It was very creative. It was a fun conversation. Jim Smith was definitely "attractive" in all ways to me. However, he always seemed so much older and mature than me. After all, he was an upperclassman!

However, in the next couple of weeks we were "running into" one another much more. We'd see each other in the halls more and exchange our high energy "hellos". We sat opposite each other during chapel in the balcony. He, with all of his upperclassmen "cool" friends and I, with my friends. I'd sneak little looks over to him and see that he was looking so I'd give a little smile or nod and I'd get one back. I realized this guy was very handsome and between the "hellos" and the "looks", I really thought he was great! I would get really excited when we'd leave chapel and more and more, we seemed to be leaving the same way so we'd talk and laugh all the way out!

Well, now we were talking. She would recognize me in the hallways and during chapel, we would actually notice each other, but more like I would stare at her until she turned her head in my direction and then I would look away. Perhaps I would then turn toward her and she would notice me and then smile. I never wanted her to know much I would just look at her. Of course my seat that I chose to sit at was much farther behind hers, so that I could easily see her at all times.

Fortunately she chose to sit in the balcony also. After chapel I would hurry and "accidentally" meet her on the way down the balcony stairs.

Now also at this time in my life I was getting ready to go to a homecoming week-end with a guy whom I had liked off and on for about 5 years. You know one of those romances where you'd see each other at summer camp or a church retreat and like each other, then write letters because you lived far away from each other. Then you'd just kind of stop writing until the next summer or church retreat. Steve was a great Christian guy whom I respected a lot and he was to be crowned king of his High School Homecoming court so he had called me at Moody and invited me to come to his football game Friday night and his Homecoming Dance as his escort Saturday night. It was a privilege and I was very excited but I started having these small conflicting feelings with my excitement with Jim. However, Jim wouldn't ever like me I had decided and Steve and I would have a fun weekend because we knew each other so why not go.

My only problem was I had to take the train out of Union Station in Chicago and I needed a boy to accompany me there. I immediately thought of Jim - after all he was becoming a good friend so at one of our "chance" meetings I asked him if he would be able to accompany me on the bus to the train station. I knew he worked on Fridays and I would need to leave by 4:30 p.m. to make my train in order to see Steve's football game he was playing in. If I missed the train, I'd miss the game.

Shortly afterwards, Vicki asked me if I would be able to take her to the train station the next weekend. She was going down to her home town for a homecoming celebration. I wasn't too excited about her leaving, but at least I would have another chance to be with her.

She wanted to meet me at 4:30 p.m. on Friday so we would be at the station by 5:30pm. This sounded pretty early for us to leave, since it was only a 30 minute walk and we were not going to walk. She wanted to take the bus. However, Vicki wanted to be early, so she made me promise I would be there at 4:30 p.m. in the girl's dorm lobby.

All week I made fun of the fact that she wanted to leave at 4:30. Although I promised I would be there, I made her think twice about leaving so early. I told her that I would be pushing it to get to the dorm from where I worked, but I would be there. I wanted to tease her a little, but not too much that she would end up asking someone else to take her to the train station.

The day finally arrived, and guess what? I was late! At least that is what Vicki thought. I looked at the clock in the lobby. It was 4:34. I was not concerned though, we had plenty of time to catch the bus and get to the train station. That day I found out that my little heartthrob had a temper. She was now sure that she would miss the train and it was all my fault. I shouldn't have changed her timetable. She had everything planned and I had messed it up!

Well, I smiled and told her that I thought we still could make it to the station if we hurried. We hopped on the bus and arrived in plenty of time. In fact, after we got her ticket, we sat down to rest and talk awhile! After I walked her to the gate, we said goodbye. It was a strange goodbye. We were friends, but it seemed there was more. "Something" was in the air. We never touched, no hug goodbye, no handshaking, but something was there. I hoped she would remember me all weekend at homecoming.

I knew Jim would probably have to take off early from his work, so I wanted to be sure he could do this...I really couldn't be late. He wanted to take off work and take me to the train station and PROMISED he'd be there on-

time although every time he saw me, he teased me about leaving so EARLY and that we didn't need an hour to get to the station.

He'd say, "Sure hope I'm not going to be late, then we'd only have 45 MINUTES to get there and we'd have to sit and wait there still!"

Oh wel, l I knew he was just teasing and knowing him and the great person he was, he would be there on time because he knew how important it was to me and how I counted on him.

However, on Friday, as I waited in the girl's dorm lobby, minute by minute ticked by 4:30 p.m., our promised departure time! I saw other guys picking up other girls to take them to the train station - where was he? This wasn't like him was it? Would he really forget or not be conscientious enough to follow through with what he had promised? He really let me down and I was very nervous about riding the train alone and making all my contacts. I had really put Jim up on a pedestal of not ever doing anything wrong and this really hurt.

Finally, I saw him walking slowly in to the lobby, as if everything was all right and we had all the time in the world!

He was smiling and said, "Ready to go?"

He didn't even realize he had let me down and his image had come crashing down and how frustrated and scarred I was inside! I was angry and proceeded to tell him so.

He just calmly listened and said, "I'm sorry but I really think we have enough time to make it to the train station.... let's go."

And we did - by the time I got my ticket, we STILL had time to sit and talk and I apologized for getting so upset...of course I couldn't tell him that one of the main reasons I was so upset was because he let me down. Jim, the gentleman that he was, carried my bags and walked me out all the way

71

to my train. Now it was time to say good-bye. I really didn't want to go, nor was I thinking about my week-end coming up. I turned to look at him to say good-bye and he was looking down at me so gently and caring, our eyes met and it was as if there was no one else there but us. There was this quiet "good-bye" - like no words were being said, yet a lot of feelings being felt.

Suddenly, we both snapped out of it and he said, "Bye, see you when you come back."

I floated onto the train, not because of what was ahead of me, but of what I had just left. I hung on to his words of "I'll see you when you come back". Jim Smith had left quite an impression.

That impression made consequences throughout that whole week-end with Steve. We had fun and I still thought he was a wonderful guy but once again, we were living in different places, different lives and we both realized it as we said good-bye on Sunday morning at the train station. This good-bye was completely different and I was excited about the "hello" coming up. However, I knew I wouldn't see Jim right away - he had to teach a Sunday School class for Chinese children on Sunday afternoons, so a couple of my girl friends met me at the station and I paid for a taxi cab to get back to Moody. But very soon that "hello" or "chance" meeting would come.

Sure enough the next morning there was a cute wrapped up note from Jim in my mail box, apologizing again and hoping I had a good time on my weekend. Then I received a phone call from Jim asking if I wanted to "sub" for him on a tour and make some extra money.

"Sure" I said, a little disappointed because this brought me back to earth reminding me that we really just worked at the same place and he was good at his job of public relations with people. I had probably only imagined he was interested in me because I wanted him to be. The plans were to meet on

72

a Thursday after they were closed down, so Jim could give me a sample "tour" so I would know exactly what to do. It was fun and he was very cute...he even seemed a little flirty but I told myself it was probably just my imagination again. Anyway, I wasn't going to date anymore anyway

Oh yeah I didn't tell you what decision I had come to after my week-end with Steve, some bad dates at Moody and my conflicting feelings for Jim. I told the Lord I was really just tired of "dating" for fun. I was only eighteen so I wasn't ready to "date" for marriage. I decided I was just going to say "no" to every guy who asked me out from then on, and if or when God wanted me to date my future "mate" He would have to do it without me realizing that it was happening. I really had just come to the conclusion that God loved me and I wanted Him in charge of my dating life. I was very serious and wanted to be held accountable to saying "no", so I shared it with my roommate and a few close friends.

Of course, God allowed me to be challenged right away. That night after I had shared this decision with some of my friends, boy after boy from Moody started calling me to ask me out for the week-end. These were really great guys, but I answered every one with a "no". I didn't give an excuse, just a thanks for asking, but "no." This started to become almost a marathon or a joke because I'd get off the phone and it would ring again. My roommate began to count and by the last phone call, she reported to me that I had declared THIRTEEN no answers in that one night!

Wow - to me I thought God was really testing my decision and if I would stand firm. (Or that someone found out and just had all these guys call, except they were all different kind of guys and different years in school...hmm) It was a little hard because there were some really neat guys, but I felt a peace because I felt like now my "dating" life was out of my hands and into God's hands. It also was very flattering to my self esteem that thirteen guys wanted to go out with me!

Following our trip to the station, I started to get brave and sent her little notes to her via the mailbox. Silly things like little paper animals that I learned to make, like a paper frog, and then I would write a short message like, "And this is what I learned to make in chapel today."

The next weekend I was going to visit my home and I needed someone to fill in my job as a tour guide on Friday afternoon. Vicki had now found herself as a part-time tour guide, and so I asked my boss if it would be alright if Vicki could take my tour on Friday afternoon. Ken said it would be fine, as long as I instructed her on how to lead this particular tour. Fine with me, more time with Vicki. I called her and asked if she wanted to make some extra money and help me out at the same time. She agreed to meet me on Thursday so I could take her on a personal tour of Moody. I curiously asked her if anyone asked her out yet. She smiled and said that just last night, thirteen guys called her for a date. Her roommate was counting. She said no to all thirteen. Well, I wasn't going to be joining in the competition this week, so I changed the subject and moved on with the tour.

Anyway back to Jim and the "tour" he was giving me to prepare me to be a tour guide. As we come to this one place he sat up on a desk and asked me how I was doing after one month at Moody and finally asked me if I had been on a lot of dates.

"No." I replied.

"You're kidding!" he said

I knew what was ahead...I think he was working up to asking me out. 'Okay, Lord, even Jim, number 14' I thought to myself.

"You mean no one has asked you out?"

"Well, yes," I answered. "In fact, now that you brought it up, just last night thirteen guys asked me out. My roommate counted them, but I said no to them all"

"Oh that's nice." Jim said.

And that was it. He got up and proceeded to take me on the tour as if nothing happened. I couldn't believe it. He didn't ask me out. He led up to it I thought but didn't say a word. Why didn't he want to ask me out? Oh well, now I knew for sure - He was a great, good-looking guy who really only liked me as a friend - nothing more. I was a little disheartened, but really I new this was for the better. I had made a big decision with God and He knew what He was doing.

I did Jim's tour and when he returned, he had to keep calling me to make a place to meet after a class or something so I could give him back his keys that I used for the tour. He now needed those keys back. We either missed each other or I'd forget the keys, so finally after two full days of work without his keys, Jim called me on a Tuesday evening and said he was waiting in the women's lounge area in the lobby for me to bring down his keys if I could. That way I wouldn't miss him anymore

I was busy studying so I came down the elevator in my socks even and found Jim sitting on a couch in the lobby. I sat to talk for a minute and we ended up talking until the women=s lounge closed. So much for studying!!

Every night after that Jim would call me and we would talk. I could tell him just about everything including my decision with the Lord about my dating situation. Jim was making a great impression...in fact he was becoming my best friend at Moody Bible Institute.

These calls with Jim would make my day and the notes, the looks, the "hi's" the "chance" meetings became more and more frequent until my friends pointed out to me that he was giving me lots of attention.

"Oh, we're just really good friends!" would be my reply to their teasing. I just thought he liked me as a "little sister" because he always seemed so mature; maybe I thought he was just too good or "cool" for me. I don't know exactly

what I was thinking except that I really enjoyed my time with him and always looked forward to the next time

I did continue the notes in her mailbox and her friends thought that it was cute. It is always good to have the friends think you're cute. It was good positive peer influence. So I kept it going. After chapel or in the dinning room she would often thank me for the little notes. I realize that constant attention and little things mean much to a girl, especially if she could tell one of her friends about it. Friend approval was important , and I was beginning to be approved. In fact, I was getting approval from Vicki's good friend who often sat next to Vicki in chapel. Her name was Jeannie.

For the longest time I really could figure out who I liked better, Jeannie or Vicki. Jeannie mentioned to Vicki that she would be interested in going out with me sometime, so Vicki told me that I should ask Jeannie out. A sure date with a pretty girl was sounding good, so I asked Jeannie out.

Jeannie and I had a good time and we went out on several dates. I took her walks along the Chicago lakefront, went out for some food, and I even introduced her to my dad while we were at a church service. We were friends, but that was about all I felt toward Jeannie. We never kissed or even held hands. She became a friend.

While we were going out, I found it difficult not to talk about one common interest between us, Vicki. Almost always I would come home from a date with Jeannie and call, not Jeannie, but Vicki, and tell her about our time together. Jeannie would come down to Vicki's room and also discuss the date with her. She got both sides of the fence about each date.

One particular time, while I was waiting for Jeannie to come down from her room in the lobby of the girl's dorm, Vicki came down to help me pass the time. A thrill went through me as we talked. I looked intently into her eyes, not wanting to look away and not embarrassed that I was looking so intently at her. She in turn kept her eyes on mine, and we talked in our own little world. In fact, when Jeannie arrived, she had to interrupt our conversation. Jeannie was sensing that I was not interested in pursuing her much farther than just friends and told Vicki that I still talked about her on the dates. Vicki just laughed it off and said we were good for one another.

One day my good friend Jeannie said she really thought Jim Smith was good looking and wanted to go out with him. I liked Jeannie a lot and thought the world of my best friend, Jim so I mentioned it one night on one of Jim's and my phone calls. All of a sudden he started smiling and waving at Jeannie at chapel, put notes in her mail box and then started taking her out. To be truthful, I was happy for them but really sad inside.

"I'm probably sad because I miss his attention," I thought. "And that's childish...I should be happy for them- not jealous of Jeannie. They were a cute couple and she really liked him."

One time that stands out in my mind was when I saw Jim waiting in the lounge for Jeannie one night. I went in to sit with him and talk until she came. He was so handsome and so fun and all of a sudden our eyes met again, like before at the train station, in our own world. What was he doing? Didn't he like Jeannie or does he like me? I didn't know but I loved looking into his eyes and him looking deeply into mine.

Then Jeannie came in and said, "Hi guys, oh thank you so much Jim for the frog note. It's so cute."

"Frog note?" I thought. "Hey, he only makes those frog notes for me. He puts them in MY mail box and now he's putting them in HERS!" I had to get out of there so I said good bye and had tears go down my cheeks all the way to the tenth floor on the elevator. I had to get control of

myself. He was now her boyfriend and I had to realize that he liked her. This was good, wasn't it? Then why did I feel so bad and sad?

Vicki wasn't just sitting around in her room while I was off on dates with one of her best friends, but she was dating some guys herself. As we talked on the phone, she would tell me about this date she had and where they went.
Some dates were fun, and deep down inside me I didn't like those guys. Some of her dates were bad and I would actually have to counsel her afterwards. All the while, our friendship was growing.

After one particular date with Jeannie, however, things got a little touchy between Vicki and Jeannie. And it was my fault. As usual I was calling Vicki after my date with Jeannie. As usual Jeannie was coming into Vicki's room to talk. Both happened at the SAME time. Jeannie figured who was on the phone and left the room. Vicki told me that she had to go and talk to Jeannie. Oops! It was looking that instead of having two girls that liked me, now I had none.

The next day was Sunday and Vicki and I were walking to church, a habit we started since we found out that we both were going to the same church. Vicki had a message from Jeannie. She did not want to go out with me anymore. Now it always hurts when someone says no more in a dating relationship, but we were still friends and I really couldn't decide on whether I liked Vicki or Jeannie better. Dating Jeannie had helped somewhat, but now Jeannie seemed to "unknowingly redirect all my efforts toward Vicki. Could she be the one?

After Jim would take Jeannie out on dates, he would call me up no matter how late and tell me all they did on their dates. I would try to help him understand Jeannie better. She was a deep thinker, kind of a poet thinker. Anyway one night

Jeannie came to my room after one of her dates with Jim and the phone rang. It was Jim. I was very uncomfortable with this because Jeannie was just telling me about her doubts of Jim's affections for her because she thought he really deep down liked me. I was reassuring her that Jim and I were just friends, but here he was on the phone with me and she was on my bed pouring out her soul. Jeannie guessed it was Jim on the phone by my look of uneasiness and ran out of my room and slammed the door.

"Jim, this is not good. I can't talk to you now. Jeannie was here and I know your call to me has upset her!"

He said he was sorry, but he had one question, "Was I still going to walk with him to church tomorrow morning as usual?"

"Sure," I answered," now bye!" He was really funny I thought. Here was the girl he liked really upset and he just wanted to know if we were walking to church together still. We had been doing this for a few weeks every Sunday morning, night and Wednesday night once we found out that we both went to Moody church. After all we were good friends and it was fun walking together.

Well I went to Jeannie's room and she really wasn't mad. She said she had made a decision and she wanted me to be her messenger to Jim. I didn't like the sound of this. She decided she wasn't going to date Jim anymore. I told her I couldn't tell him that because it would make him feel very bad. She said she really didn't want to tell him and since I was his good friend, it would be easier for him if I told him.

"Besides," she said, "I really think he likes you. He's always talking about you so I really don't want to date him anymore, because he likes you, Vicki."

"No, we're just very good friends. That's ridiculous!" I answered.

Nevertheless, the next morning I found myself walking to church with Jim, trying to think of the best or easiest way to break the news to him. He was so nice and I was sure he was to be crushed. I really didn't want to do this. I told Jim, Jeannie's message, and waited for the expected sadness.

But instead without a beat he replied, "Great, that's my answer!" and he proceeded with our everyday conversation.

I didn't understand this reaction. Perhaps he had been praying whether or not to date Jeannie. Whatever had just happened surprised me, but I was happy that Jim wasn't crushed!

The next week was Mission's Conference and one night on the phone as Jim and I were talking, he said that he knew who the speaker was on Thursday night and gave me the speaker's name. I laughed because I knew that the speaker he was talking about was preaching Thursday afternoon, not Thursday night. So we bet each other that the loser (the one who wasn't right) needed to treat the other one to a pizza dinner at East Inn. Jim, of course lost and I was to receive a free dinner on Friday night.

As I got ready for this dinner on Friday night, I realized there were other girls on my floor who were getting ready for dates that night and I looked a lot like them, getting ready for a date. I was assuring myself, "this wasn't a date, just a paid-back bet". I felt a little nervous...maybe this wasn't good because it didn't go along with my decision about dating. Oh what was I worried about...we were just best friends!

When I saw Jim, he put my mind at ease and we had a wonderful time! This best friend of mine was certainly making an impression on me!

As September moved into October, our school would cancel classes from a week and hold a missionary conference. This was a welcome break for studies and a good time to hear some good missionary speakers and consider the future. It also provided a great way to get a date with Vicki.

We saw each other sometime early in the week, and the discussion came up about one of the special speakers that would be there later in the week. I thought one way, she thought the other way, and so to prove our point we bet a pizza dinner at East Inn, the same pizza place we went to last year when she came up to Moody to visit. The loser had to buy the dinner. I lost, but not really I got a date with Vicki. Actually, we didn't call it a date, it was just a payment on a bet.

Our time at the restaurant went well, but it was after dinner that proved to be one of the more embarrassing moments of my life. Originally we had tried to sit where we had sat the first time we came to this restaurant together, but the booth was occupied. We ate and talked and just before we left, Vicki wanted to see if we could see our names that we had carved into the booth on our first visit.

The booth was still occupied, but Vicki insisted that we should go over and ask them if we could look for our names. She was right. They didn't mind. In fact they helped us look for our names. I saw them first, but didn't say anything. I had forgotten what I wrote and now I didn't want anyone else to see what we wrote. Too late. "Vicki and JimBob". Why did I write JimBob? I don't know, but there it was and here I was. I even had bib overalls on, so I looked the part. The whole table saw my predicament and caught the giggle bug from Vicki and started to laugh with her. Red faced and all, It was pretty funny, I guess.

Well, at least Vicki was enjoying her time with me. I hoped we would have more time together.

It was a start. It wasn't perfect, but it started something that I wanted to continue.

With time and honesty, we were making good,
no I would say GREAT impressions and only
wanting to see and learn more about each other.
We were no longer attempting to make impressions,
but genuinely interested in KNOWING
the other person more and more. This was
actually easy and very fun!

I don't mean to say that I have already achieved
these things or that I have already reached
perfection! But I keep working toward that day
when I will finally be all that Christ Jesus saved
me for and wants me to be. No, dear brothers
and sisters, I am still not all I should be, but I
am focusing all my energies on this one thing:
Forgetting the past and looking forward to what
lies ahead, I strain to reach the end of the race and
receive the prize for which God, through Christ
Jesus, is calling us up to heaven.
Philippians 3:12-14

Chapter 8

"The Official Date"

～∕∕～

Building a relationship takes time and determination. It also needs to have some movement one way or the other. Either you are drifting apart or drawing closer together. We need to become a little more obvious in our intentions and the opportunities to do so present themselves, if we are observant. Somewhere along the line, we need to decide to take the risk with our heart and allow God to take care of the rest.

Building a relationship also takes "gut wrenching" honesty; mostly with yourself. You need to ask yourself the right questions. Do you really want this relationship or not? Are you willing to honestly pursue or investigate the possibility of this relationship? Are you just playing a part or maybe you are just too worried about what other people think. You need to be able to weigh out all the facts and feelings and get to your real heart. No games, no lying to oneself or others. Here's how we got to "the official date"…

We were having a good time and soon I found myself writing silly little notes to Vicki all the time. I would call her often and talk for a long time. I wanted to spend time with her and she was fast becoming my best friend.

One weekend Vicki flew across Lake Michigan with Jeannie to her home in Michigan. Jeannie's dad was a pilot, and flew them home for a time of rest and relaxation. I have always wanted to fly in a small plane, but Vicki didn't think it was that fun.

While she was away for the weekend, I started to notice that many guys were getting a date for our fall banquet. I had thought about it a little bit, and since I still had three weeks to go, I thought I had plenty of time. I found out that most girls would like at least a week's notice for a big date, and three weeks isn't out of the question. Now, with everyone, or at least it seemed to me everyone, getting a date for the fall banquet, I started to worry that someone would ask Vicki to the banquet before I got the chance. It was a good thing she was away, since nobody could ask her, but as soon as she came back, I decided I would pop the big question. It was at the time, the big question. It seems that the next important question is always the "BIG question"!

The problem was that although I knew she would be coming back Sunday night, I had no idea what time. Maybe someone would ask her before I got the chance. I would die if that happened.

I told my friends about getting a date for the banquet and they all wanted to know who I was going to ask. They actually got together in my room to hear what I would say on the phone when I called her. They had piles of suggestions. Some good, some dumb. I dialed her number and told them to be quiet.

Finally, after what seemed like twenty rings, an out-of-breath Vicki came to the phone. She had just arrived from Michigan and had heard the phone ringing as she got off the elevator and said her uncle was down in the lobby waiting for her and she had to get going. I said I understood and then I did it. I popped the "big question!"

"Oh, by the way, would you like to go with me to the fall banquet?"

"Oh, by the way" I heard myself say. What kind of question was this? I made it sound like an afterthought, when it was the only reason I had called. Why did I do that?

Vicki answered, "I don't know, but my uncle is waiting for me in the lobby so I'm in a hurry, I'll call you back."

As I hung up, everyone wanted to know what she said. I told them she had to hurry and see her uncle in the lobby and she'll call me back later. They all laughed and the consensus was to look for someone else. When a girl says, "I don't know," that means she hasn't figured out how to say no yet. I didn't want to look for someone else, so I said I would wait for her return call. Anyway, we were good friends by now and I was sure Vicki would say yes. Why wouldn't she?

I had a great weekend with Jeannie and her family and the added new experience of flying in a small airplane with Jeannie's dad as a pilot. I was apprehensive at first but Jim encouraged me that it was an experience of a lifetime! He was right!

My uncle and aunt saw me in the girl's lobby as I arrived home. They were taking me to a concert here at Moody, so I told them I would take my luggage upstairs to my room and then be right back down so as to get a good seat.

As I was getting off the elevator, I heard my phone ringing. It was Jim just calling to talk. As kindly as I could I told him I had to go so he fit this question in at the end that blew my night apart.

"By the way," he said, "Would you like to go with me to the fall banquet?"

I didn't have time to digest this, so I quickly explained my situation with going to the concert, and said "I'll call you back". Whew! Off the hook for now. All through the concert I thought about what to answer Jim. I wanted to go because I knew we would have a great time together, and Jim would be the only one I would want to go with, but this was awfully close to a date to other people and I had told God I would say "no". What was I to do? I knew that Jim and I could go to the banquet as good friends but everyone else would think it's a date and get the wrong idea. I would have to say "no" even thought I wished I could say "yes".

I was very nervous to call Jim. I hardly ever called boys. My parents never wanted me to call boys. Jim had always called me, however I told him that I would call him back, so I must. I probably picked up the phone a dozen times only to hang it up in a panic. I finally took a deep breath and dialed his number expecting Jim to answer. The phone was answered, but it was by Steve, Jim's roommate. This really mixed me up. I had my speech all prepared to say "no" so Jim would understand. But this wasn't Jim. I responded by "Oh, hi Steve. Is Jim there?"

"No."

That was not the answer I was looking for and only served to mix me up more. I may have begun to say something, but the silence was terrible and Steve is a very direct person. He wasn't going to beat around the bush with this.

"Is this Vicki?" he asked.

"Yes".

"Are you calling Jim back about the banquet?"

"Yes".

"Well are you going to go with him?"

I was so frantic by now that I didn't stop to think this wasn't his business and I should ask him to have Jim call me back. My immediate reaction was to just answer.

"No, I'm not going with him to the banquet. We're good friends but I think others wouldn't understand."

Very loudly and without a hint of apology, Steve disciplined me, "You're a jerk? How could you say no to him. You two talk on the phone every night. You're just too worried about what others will say instead of concerned about how this will make Jim feel! I'm not telling him your answer. You have to call him and tell him yourself!"

Click. Dead silence. The lecture was over and I felt sick inside.

He was right! I was a jerk! Here Jim and I had become best friends and because of what others would think, I was going to hurt our relationship. What was I thinking? It didn't matter what others thought. This wasn't a date, just a fun time with a great friend.

So, later that evening I called him. What if Steve had told Jim of our call? What would he think of me now? If I thought I was nervous before, I was extremely anxious now.

When he answered he sounded happy that it was me, asked me again about my weekend in Michigan and how the concert was with my aunt and uncle. Good, good, good! How was I going to bring this up? Then he asked me again.

"So, will you accompany me to the fall banquet?"

"Yes". There I said it.

"Good, we'll have a great time."

I really don't know anything else that was said. I was just relieved!

Some time later she did call back, and I nervously asked her again if she would like to accompany me to the fall banquet. She said she would and then after a short conversation we hung up. I turned to my roommate and he asked if that was Vicki who called. I said yes. He asked me what she said. I told him, with a big smile on my face, that she said yes. Then he got this huge "I know something you don't know" smile on his face and I asked him why the smile.

He simply said, "I'll tell you after the banquet!"

No big deal, I thought Vicki was going to say yes anyway, so I didn't dwell on what Steve was smiling about. I let it go. I was happy, Vicki was going with me to the banquet.

As the banquet got closer, Vicki and I spent more time on the phone and seeing each other around the campus. We still didn't go out on a date, but we started to spend more time together. We were still just good friends and Vicki still had another guy who liked her from the past summer, who was coming up to visit her on the weekend of the banquet.

I was calm about this visit, confident that Vicki and I had a strong enough relationship and friendship that could stand up to outside pressures, but we still were only good friends and my jealousy and worries flared up a bit with this guy coming to town.

In fact, some of my friends came up to my room and mentioned that they had seen Vicki talking to some guy down in the lounge area. This guy also had a guitar, and was playing some songs. Major weakness! I don't play the guitar. I don't play anything and I only sing so-so.

My good buddy and roommate, Steve told me that he was going to go down and check this new guy out. Steve knew much about our friendship, since he had often heard the one sided phone conversations that Vicki and I had most every night. In fact, if we talked too late into the night, he would strongly suggest that I take the phone call into the hallway. So, knowing my fears and a little apprehensions, he went on down to the lobby.

I'll never forget what he said when he came back. "Smith, you have nothing to worry about!"

So I didn't worry. Although she was going to be with some other friends from her home town tonight, including this guy, the banquet was tomorrow night and I was going with the girl of my dreams.

I did all the right things. I got some flowers, made sure I knew what color dress she was wearing so the flowers would match, arranged to meet with some other couples so the conversations would be easy and told Vicki where and when I would meet her for the banquet.

When I arrived at the girl's dorm, all the guys in the school seemed to be there with the same idea. We all wanted to be early so we could get a good seat in the dining room. Well, time was on my side, so I wasn't worried. Paul was one of my friends who I was going to double date with later on in the evening. We were waiting together for our dates. Paul's date came first and after a while, we thought it would be best if they went to get a place in line. Good idea.

Other girls came and met their dates and took off for the dining room. It was now well past our scheduled meeting time and I was one of the few remaining guys in the lobby. In fact, some guys came in, waited for their dates, and left while I was still waiting. I thought about calling, but I didn't want to come across too demanding, so I waited. And I waited some more. I started to think that maybe something was wrong.

Finally, the elevator doors opened and there stood my date for the evening. She looked great and we were now starting our official first date. I gave her the flowers and wisked her off to the dining room, hoping our friends had saved a spot for us.

The weekend of the banquet was going to be very busy. I had friends coming in on Friday night and Saturday morning and then on Saturday at noon, another girl and I had to take a bus to the flower store and then come home to get ready.

The meeting with friends went fine and of course, my girlfriend and I got lost looking for the flower shop, so by the time we got home, I had a half hour before meeting Jim downstairs. Now, one must note that even a short period of time for a girl to get ready for this kind of social occasion would be at least one hour. As I walked onto my floor, I saw many girls all dressed up and ready to go and here I was wind blown and in my jeans with no make up on. "Oh well, I don't have to look really good," I thought, "because we can't have too much fun and start liking each other, because we can't date anyway. Liking each other would only ruin our relationship, but when I saw all the other girls getting so dressed up, I decided I'd better shower and try to look decent. However, I started to feel more nervous again about what people would think. it was getting later and later and I didn't know what to do. Maybe I should just call Jim and tell him that I couldn't do this; no, I couldn't do that...that would be mean and unkind. I had to go, but I'd better make sure that neither he nor I had too much fun. Coming down late would probably start things off poorly. I'm sure Jim was getting a little upset that I wasn't sticking to the plan (I remembered me with the train date).

When I got off the elevator I expected a "Finally!" or "Nice you could make it" or some sarcastic remark.

Instead, Jim smiled and said, "You look great! Here I got this for you." and he proceeded to hand me a beautiful corsage. Now this was impressive. He wasn't mad at all. He was simply happy to see me. In fact when we found his friends who were saving us a place in line, he didn't even blame me. He just apologized for "our" lateness. He had nothing to do with "our" lateness and yet didn't publicly embarrass me. Stop it. I couldn't have this much admiration or adoration for him.

During dinner, we had a great time. In fact, I talked more than I usually do. Maybe I was nervous, but when I commented that everyone at our table was eating so fast,

Vicki blurted out that it wasn't that they were eating so fast, but that I was talking so much, I didn't have time to eat.

"Just kidding", she said.

Funny. I did start to eat more and talk less then.

Later on, Vicki commented on the inside scoop of all these girls who were sitting with guys they didn't want to go with to the banquet, but they just did it to be nice. She would point to a couple on one side of the dining room and then swing over to the other side. So it seemed like everyone didn't want to go with whom they were sitting with at the banquet.

I looked at her and said, "Well I'm glad you wanted to go with me? Didn't you?"

"No!" she said. Then she added, "Just kidding!"

"Ha, ha, very funny," I thought, but this was not helping me feel real great. The thought was planted. Did she or didn't she?

As we sat and ate our dinner, Jim talked a lot in order to keep the conversation going. After awhile Jim looked at our friends plates and then commented that our plates were empty and his was still full!

"Well if somebody wouldn't be talking so much, their plate would probably be empty also!" This sarcastic unkind remark slivered through my lips. It's one of those statements that you wish you could take back as soon as you hear yourself saying it. Of course, as soon as it was said, I saw Jim's look of defeat. I saw the hurt in his eyes and embarrassment.

"I'm just kidding." There. I thought that would fix the lashings of my tongue, but Jim quieted down and ate his dinner while I decided to take over the dinner conversation and began to point out all the girls who didn't want to be with the dates they were with.

Jim was really surprised but smirked and said, "Well, I'm glad you wanted to go with me, didn't you?"

"No" ...there I went again and saw that it hurt him again.

Not that he pouted or anything; I just could see it in his eyes so I quickly added on, "Just kidding!" (The great "fixer" statement to cover all ills or truths too hard to come to grips with!)

After the banquet, we planned to go to the suburbs of Chicago with Paul and his date and go bowling and maybe get dessert at some restaurant .after in the evening. I borrowed my father's VW beetle and arranged to meet our dates near the parking lot. Just to impress the girls, I drove my car through a tunnel to meet the girls. They were impressed, until I found out that the reverse gear did not work and I, with Vicki's help, had to push the car backwards all the way out of the tunnel. But it did start the night off on a lighter side. It was funny.

On the way to the bowling lanes, I decided to stop in and visit my family. They were having a birthday party for my brother and I wanted to drop in and wish him a Happy Birthday. It also would be a good time for them to meet Vicki.

As we were eating birthday cake, I was standing up and trying to be careful not to spill any crumbs on the floor. I guess I had the cake too close to my face for Vicki to resist the temptation of pushing the entire piece of cake into my face!

This was the first time my mom had met Vicki and I wondered how she was going to react to Vicki stuffing cake into her firstborn's face.

She burst out with a laugh and said, "I've always wanted to do that to Jim!"

Well, now my family likes her. It was worth a cake in the face.

When I went back to my dorm room to change to casual clothes so we could go out bowling, I couldn't believe I had been so mean. What's wrong with me? I'm back to being too worried about what others thought. It would be nice that we were going off campus for the rest of the night because then I could relax more.

The time at Jim's family's home for his brother's birthday was really fun. It was Jim and me just having fun being friends. As we were standing around talking and eating our cake, I couldn't believe that I pushed Jim's plate of cake into his face right in front of his family. I think because he held it so close up to his face that it was a bit too tempting and he looked so cute. He took it well and we all laughed. His family was a lot of fun and loving; of course, what should I expect? This night was really becoming lots of fun. I was now glad that I had decided to go on this "non-date" with Jim.

Bowling went well. In fact, it went really well. Vicki beat me I think, but I didn't really care because every time she got a strike or a spare on her score, she would come up to me and teasingly tap me. Then I would gently push her aside and tell her that this time I was going to get the strike. The highlight of the evening was the casual touch we shared throughout the game. It wasn't for more than a second, but it sent a chill up and down my spine that made me shiver. How I wish we would always get that thrilled from the little things in life. We are so rushed to get on with other things. We need to just enjoy each aspect of dating, to never tire of the simple.

I didn't want to rush things, so flirting was all we did that night. But it was fun. Later we went to a restaurant for dessert. Vicki wanted to see the pictures in my wallet. As she paged through them, she stopped and looked at the picture of my girlfriend. I had forgotten to take it out of my wallet.

She looked puzzled. She asked me who this girl was and I told her. Then a smile came on her face and she looked like she just solved a puzzle. In fact she did!

She said that this girl, a stranger to her, but now it made sense, had come up to look at her room occasionally, and always seemed to ask strange questions. I smiled and also told Vicki that she had moved in to the same room that my former girlfriend was in last year. In fact, for the past two years I had been calling two different girls, but using the same telephone number.

Vicki now was looking jealous, just a little, which I didn't mind seeing, but I let the subject drop. So far, so good.

The ride home however turned into a most uncomfortable, but then again, comical memory. Not only did the reverse stick shift not work in the car, but the radio did not work as well. The other couple who was along with us was crammed in the back seat of the VW. Halfway home, Vicki and I noticed that the talking had quit in the back seat. I looked in the rearview mirror and found out that there was quite a lot of kissing going on in the back seat.

I told Vicki not to look, but of course whenever anyone says that, everyone looks. Vicki looked and almost started to laugh. I did too, since it looked like the most unromantic place in the world to be kissing. Instead of listening to them kissing all the way back to Moody, we decided to start singing. We sang camp songs, church songs, top 40 songs, made-up songs all the way back to school.

By the time we were bowling, we wee back to flirting and even soft touches of encouragement. I really thought Jim was a great guy and actually maybe for the first time thought he actually liked me a little...all in all it was a great night. Too bad it hadn't ended here!

After I walked Vicki to her dorm and said good night, I smiled and considered the night a smashing success. Tomorrow, Vicki and I would go to church together as usual, which would give me another day with Vicki. The only cloud in my sky that night was the one I was flying on.

God wants us to enjoy life. He sets boundaries
around us to protect and guide us. If we stay
within those limitations, with God's help,
life becomes filled with more joy.

Their trust should be in the living God,
whom we need for our enjoyment.
I Timothy 6:17

My purpose is to give life in all its fullness.
John 10:10

Chapter 9

The First Kiss

∾

Taking it slowly in the physical area is a good way to build relationships. Unfortunately many tend to think that a passionate physical relationship is a good relationship. This is not necessarily true. Some think that getting a kiss on the first date is a good sign. Again, going slowly is a better way to build a relationship. Becoming too physical will overtake the desire to learn about the emotional, mental and spiritual side of the other person. Take your time. The physical will come. However, the physical seems to be an ongoing, ever-present thought and although I was willing to wait, it was on my mind.

I was always taught that a true gentleman always waits for the lady and is respectful of her when it comes to the physical part of their relationship. I was also taught that if a man truly loves you, he is more than willing to wait for you. So....

After Jim dropped me off at my dorm, I really realized that I had a great time and to be honest was starting to like Jim more than just a best friend. I wasn't quite sure what to do with these feelings or even if they were wise or not when my phone rang. It was the girl who had been kissing Paul all the way home from bowling. She was crying and wondered if I could come down to her room and talk to her.

When I got to her room, between sobs she was so sorry for what she had done (I agreed because it was even her first date with Paul). However, to make matters worse, she didn't even really have feelings for him. I couldn't believe it. How could she have done this and not even liked him as a boyfriend? She had truly wronged Paul by acting one way, but not truly knowing her feelings for him. In the middle of my thoughts, I realized that perhaps in the same way I had wronged Jim. I had acted pretty flirty, but still was not sure of my feelings or if my feelings were right. How dare I judge this girl. We decided she must tell Paul the truth and apologize to him for her behavior. Great! Her problem was solved, but my predicament had only become more confusing. I felt sick to my stomach and couldn't sleep all night.

By morning, I really needed more time to think and didn't feel well. I knew I couldn't face Jim yet because I didn't know what to think myself yet, so once again, I had to call him. I told him I wasn't feeling very well so I wouldn't be accompanying him to church that morning as usual. (I did have that sick sort of feeling in the pit of my stomach).

He said, "All right." I knew he was confused but not anymore than I was.

I slept in that morning and then got up to go and eat Sunday lunch. I timed my lunch so as not to see Jim yet in the lunchroom. I needed to know how I really felt about him before seeing him. My heart and my head could not find an answer.

The next morning I'm ready to go to church with Vicki, but this time it would be special. We now had a mutual liking of one another. Last night was going to be the building block of a great relationship. I couldn't wait to see Vicki again.

And then the bomb exploded. It seems we often get hurt when we least expect it. Becoming transparent and opening yourself up to another human being can bring great joy, but also great pain. It is a risk most people wisely take. I took it and got burned. The call came Sunday morning. Vicki said she wasn't feeling well and she decided not to go to church with me that morning. I said I understood and hung up.

I may have been a little confused at that time, but my anger brewed inside of me and overcame my confusion. I was getting the short end of the stick. Vicki was lying to me. She had to be. Nothing was wrong with her last night. She must of thought about our time together and decided we were going too fast, although we weren't going as fast as our friends were. I thought through the night and couldn't figure out what went wrong. We had a great time, at least I thought, so what was the problem?

I looked at myself in the mirror of our huge bathroom in the dorm and tried to figure it out. I was lost, rejected, alone, and totally confused. I knew that Vicki had always liked my mustache and every time I wanted to shave it off, she convinced me to keep it. Now, as I looked into the mirror, I decided this would be a good time to shave off my mustache. So I did, partly because I always wanted to, and partly because I was angry at Vicki for not being honest with me and telling me why she really didn't want to go with me to church. I walked to church alone that Sunday. It was very cloudy.

The next week was awful. I knew I had hurt Jim. He didn't even look at me during chapel, in the lunchroom, never called me, and no more notes in my mail box. How could I blame him after how I had treated him. I really messed him... in fact I realized that I really cared about him and enjoyed our relationship, in fact had gotten use to having him around. What had I done? What had I communicated to Jim? What had I so easily thrown away?

One night, a couple of my friends asked me if I wanted to go down to the "Coffee Cove" (a little snack shop in the basement for students to go to hang out and eat at night.) I thought this would be a good idea to get out of my room instead of waiting for the phone to ring.

After we got our ice cream sundaes, we sat down at a table and clear across the room at a table sat Jim with another girl; a really fun, cute freshman. They were looking at their notebooks, laughing and talking. Now I really knew that any hope I had with Jim was gone. He had easily moved on, which I really didn't blame him for. She was a great girl, but I felt like my whole insides were being ripped apart. My confusion was over. I really did like and care for this man. I didn't care if everyone knew anymore. How could I tell him? It really wasn't fair of me to call him up, now that he was interested in someone else, and tell him I was mistaken. I really do like you. I miss you. I want you in my life. No. I just had to face it. I had driven off one of the best things in my life. Only one thing had I been right about..that dating hurt my relationship with my best friend. Even being right about that wasn't very consoling. Now was time for remorse and tears. I had made my bed, now I needed to lie in it. I really missed Jim!

Throughout the next week I really couldn't look at Vicki. I didn't call her, talk to her or write little notes for her mail box either. We didn't break up, because we were never really together. I still wasn't too sure what went wrong, but I wasn't in the mood to find out. Not yet. She didn't seem too anxious to track me down and explain it all to me either. But I did miss her. I drifted through that week like a canoe slowly slicing through the some cold water on a foggy day.

Somehow I wanted to talk to her. I thought that perhaps she was nervous about us becoming a couple at school, but I wanted to let everyone know how I felt about her. This would also keep other possible suitors away from her. This week however, I figured I would give Vicki the space she might have thought she needed. I wanted her to know what life was without me. If that was what she wanted, then that would have to be what it was going to be. I would give it a week, but then I would call her. I waited until Thursday night.

So on Thursday night I finally called her. My stomach was in knots, because I didn't know what she would say. I didn't even know if she wanted to talk to me. I still was angry with her for not going to church with me or being honest with me, but my desire to be with her made me overcome my anger.

Thursday night my phone rang! My heart leapt as it had every time the phone had rung in my room this week. I had trained myself to realize it wouldn't be Jim.

So when the phone would ring, my reactions would be, "Maybe? No, don't be ridiculous Vicki!"

When my room mate answered the phone, just by her tone of voice and eyes, I knew it was Jim. My heart beat rapidly, my pulse raced, my cheeks were flushed. What was he going to say? I had to act calm. I picked up the phone gingerly.

"Hello."

"Hi Vicki, this is Jim."

"Are you doing anything Friday night?"

"No."

"Would you like to baby-sit my sisters Friday night?"

"Sure."

"All right. I'll meet you in the lobby at 4:30 to take the train together to my house."

"OK."

"Bye."

"Bye."

I was so excited as I hung up the phone. He remembered me. He actually cared and asked me out. And I had immediately answered yes. I was going to see him tomorrow night! I was sure we would talk everything out then. What should I wear? It was as if it was the first time I'd ever seen him. He had to know I was interested in him now, because he knew that one of my pet peeves was when a guy asked you out only one day ahead of time. He knew I felt this was not proper or polite to the girl. Of course he had called me on Thursday night and tomorrow was Friday and I hadn't said a word about this being improper. I had not even hesitated or said I needed to check my schedule, I just quickly replied "Yes!" He must be smiling like the cat who ate the canary!

My plan was to invite Vicki to join me Friday night at my folk's home in the Chicago suburbs, since they had asked me to baby-sit my two younger sisters. I figured it would be a nice time to talk since we had at least an hour out and then an hour back to school on the train to talk. To my delight she said yes! We didn't talk long, but the time was well spent. Tomorrow I would see Vicki again!

The next day another girl, Karen, from my home town had found out that Vicki and I were going to my home on the train Friday night and she was wondering if she could join us for the trip out. (We, Karen and I had met earlier that week in the "Coffee Cove" when I was sharing some notes with another girl in my class who was friends with Karen and so as we got each other's notes we ate some ice cream together.) Karen said her folks would pick her up at the station, but it would be much safer to go out with us than alone; so I said sure.

I was very excited as I got ready to meet Jim. All of my excitement and enthusiasm came crashing down as the elevator doors opened to the lobby. There before me stood Jim and Karen, the girl whom I saw sitting with Jim in the

Friends Forever

"Coffee Cove" a few days before. My mind was reeling, but somehow I got out a "Hello".

Karen met me first in the girl's dorm lobby and shortly afterwards Vicki joined us. The three of us carried on polite conversation all the way out to the end of the line. It was pouring rain when we arrived there, but somehow Karen found her parent's car right away and thanked us of accompanying her home and then took off.

"Well, let's go." said Jim and we all three began walking to the subway station. As we walked I was trying to figure out what was happening here. However, we had to run down the stairs and quietly run into a crowded train. I found one seat by someone and Karen found a seat by someone else. Jim had to remain standing since there was not any other seat available in the train. At the next stop, the person sitting by Karen got off the train, so Jim sat by Karen. There they were again, talking and laughing together. All of a sudden the truth hit me like a brick, and my body went cold. Jim had not asked ME out on a date, but had asked me if I wanted to babysit his sisters. How could I have been so wrong? Probably he and Karen and his mom and dad were going on a double date and Jim probably said since I had met his sisters that he'd try to get a baby-sitter; after all we were friends and friends baby-sit.

My eyes stung with tears, all hope was gone, my excitement dropped to an all time low. I felt like the weather looked like outside...gray, cold, poring rain. I just tried to look out the window of the train now and watch the pouring rain come down. Once again, there was no one to blame but myself. It was too late to go back a week in our relationship. What had I thrown away? Our stop was the last stop, so we all got off the train in the pouring rain.

Then Karen excitedly said, "There's my dad. Thanks again guys for letting me come along."

Instantly, she ran off and into a waiting white car. That left Jim and me standing on the train platform in the rain, looking at one another eye to eye. This all left me totally shocked!

"I guess my dad's not here to pick us up yet," Jim commented with a small smile.

I looked at Jim and said, "So you're not going out with Karen tonight?"

"No," he laughed, beginning to see why I had been acting so strangely and seeing a glimpse of what I had been thinking.

This was a total change of direction once again, and my emotions couldn't handle anymore! Relief poured out of me by way of crying. I tried to explain to Jim what I'd been thinking on the train.

He just smiled and pulled me close to him and whispered in the softest manner, "Oh Vicki, don't you know by now that it's you I like?"

We just stood there with his arms holding me in the pouring rain, but somehow the sky didn't look dark and cold anymore. Now the rain was refreshing and warm instead of bone chilling cold.

Then the strangest time happened. Vicki asked me, with a puzzled look on her face, why I wasn't going with Karen. I laughed and simply said because I had to go baby sit my sisters. Vicki started to cry!

Suddenly it hit me that Vicki had somehow thought that she was going to baby sit my sisters while Karen and I went on a double date with my mom and dad. I smiled and simply said, "Oh Vicki, don't you know by now that it's you I like?" I reached out and just held her so she could sob her relief out. Funny how the sobs got rid of my anger also. She was just scared.

We went to my house and had a fun time baby sitting my sisters. They really liked Vicki and made her feel like she was welcomed at their home anytime. During the evening, we all sat down to watch TV and this is where Vicki and I first held hands. It was so romantic. We were sitting on the floor, with our arms crossed in front of us. As we sat shoulder to should, we also sat fingers to fingers. When our fingers touched, an electric spark flew through my body. My hands started to sweat and I forgot what program we were watching on TV. Her hand stayed where it was so I kept my fingers touching hers until they started to hurt. I was afraid to move them for fear that Vicki would move her hand away from mine, but I had to if I wanted to keep the blood circulating in my fingers.

I moved my hand towards hers, and to my surprise, she didn't move her had away. In fact, as I attempted to hold her hand, she firmly held my hand too. She even squeezed my hand a few times. We secretly held hands during the entire program, so my sisters would never know. I'm not sure why I didn't want them to know, but it was fun and just private between Vicki and me.

On the way home we had a wonderful time talking and holding hands in public. We even held hands walking down the street towards Moody, but as we got within a block of school, Vicki quit holding my hand. I didn't know why, but maybe she still didn't want anyone to see us holding hands. I didn't mind. It had been a great night, and I now had hope where there was only doubt just a few days ago.

I so enjoyed the next few weeks, having the freedom to enjoy Jim in front of everyone. We enjoyed wherever we went or whomever we were with, because of one another. We were free to allow the hidden feelings to come to the surface and be given to one another.

I realized each date we went on, perhaps Jim was getting closer and closer to looking for that first kiss. Now don't get me wrong...it wasn't that I didn't want him to kiss me...I just wanted us to take our relationship very slowly. I wanted to enjoy this stage of our dating without the pressure of when or if we should kiss. I felt the best way to take off this pressure was to have us set some boundaries. I felt a good boundary in order to take off the pressure was to agree to just not kiss until after Christmas, which was about two months away. I didn't know exactly how Jim would feel about this suggestion...however, my heart felt safe with him and I could talk to him about anything. This was and is one of the foundations of our relationship. We are safe to tell one another the truth and whatever we are thinking about because we are best friends and really only want to help the other. Many relationships are only out there for what they will get for themselves, rather than what they can give to the other. What usually happens when one feels like they have gotten all they can get out of a relationship is that they leave. However, one can never quit giving when they care about the other person more than themselves.

Another pitfall that many couples face even though they are Christians, is in their physical relationship during dating. They always want to rush it along, thinking that this is love when actually the opposite is true. True love waits and is pure and concerned about the other person's reputation.

When I presented my idea of waiting to kiss until after Christmas to Jim, he passed with flying colors when he only responded with "Sure."

It didn't seem to upset him or change the way he treated me at all. I began to believe that he really cared about my reputation and wanted to give to me and wait for me. This was a wonderful quality and we even had fun teasing with "butterfly" or "Eskimo" kisses, all the while knowing that we had promised to wait for the real kiss until after Christmas. It was understood and did take the pressure off.

The weeks flew by and we were now sitting together in chapel, eating some meals together and becoming another well established couple at Moody. I even introduced Vicki to my best friends at church and got a thumbs up from them!

We would often go on walks along Lake Michigan, or spend time sitting together in the dorm lounges just talking. We spent so much time talking late at night on the phone, that my roommate forced me to take the phone out into the hallway, so he could get some sleep!

During this time, Vicki told me that she had something very important to ask me. So I said ask me, but she wanted to do it in person. I had no idea what this would be, but I couldn't wait to hear what it was. We again took a walk along the lake, and she nervously asked me if we would wait to kiss until after Christmas, about two more months away. The idea was that this would allow us to get to know one another better and not allow us to fall into the trap of thinking we like someone just because they kissed well. It also would take the pressure off guessing whether or not we should kiss every time we went out. Should we kiss after the date, before, once, twice or all the time. Kissing is a confusing and deceptive game dating couples play, so I said "Sure."

I really enjoyed spending time with Vicki, so it wasn't going to be too difficult a promise to keep. Vicki would often test me by teasing me with butterfly kisses, putting her eye by my cheek and then blink several times, thereby making her eyelashes tickle my cheeks. We even did the Eskimo kiss, rubbing our noses together, but we never touched lips. I wouldn't do that...I had made a promise!

However, there were times that keeping this promise was unbearable. One particular time I especially remember well. It was in the Moody Memorial Church Choir room while we were waiting for my family to meet us. I was sitting on a table and Vicki was standing in front of me saying something. She stood so close to me I could smell her perfume. Her voice was giving me goose bumps all over my neck and back. A quick kiss on the cheek. I really wanted to, she was right there, but NO...I had made a promise and I was going to keep it! To her confusion, I quickly got off the table and decided to walk around the room. I had to get away from this tempting situation, yet look unaffected by her charm. Sometimes I thought it was a dumb promise, but on the other hand it made sense and made us work on our self control.

Then came Thanksgiving vacation. A short four day weekend, but a lifetime of no classes for a college student. A break from the pressure and homework and a chance to see family and friends. A good meal and a couple of days to sleep in. I was planning on going home Wednesday night, like everyone else. After the Thanksgiving service at church, I would join my family and head home to the suburbs of Chicago. Also although I only lived 25 miles away, I didn't get home enough. It was a welcomed break. Although Vicki's folks were coming up to the Chicago area to have Thanksgiving with Vicki's grandparents in North Chicago, we wouldn't see each other until after the break. We were big on spending time with our families during the holidays.

Then it happened! A freak Thanksgiving snowstorm was about to change all the best laid plans of Jim and Vicki. How would you like to spend Thanksgiving in your dormitory? Even if you can't go home, you would like to be invited over to someone's home for dinner. Wednesday nights before Thanksgiving at Moody were usually quiet ones. Most people had taken off for the break by then. Some would say that they liked the quiet, but I think they would enjoy going somewhere else if they could.

This is what I thought when Vicki called and said that her folks were caught in the blizzard and that they wouldn't be able to pick Vicki up until Thanksgiving morning at the very earliest. I made a call home and asked if Vicki could come home and wait for her parents there. It was on the way to North Chicago and when her parents finally could come they could pick her up at our house. What a great idea. Both parents thought it was a great idea too.

My dad was already at church and so after church, we got in our VW and started home. The snow was bad, but if anyone could get through a snowstorm, it was my dad. He had a little VW beetle and could drive that through just about anything. Unfortunately, Vicki sat in the passenger's seat and had a clear view of the traffic and snow. Watching my dad drive was not always comforting to strangers, however, we made it safely home, but had to pry Vicki's hands off the handle in front of her seat!

After dinner and conversation, television and games, everyone headed off in different directions. Vicki and I were alone in the living room able to talk. Now most couple's use the excuse that they need to talk, which really means that they want to kiss. Most parents know that, because they did the same thing, but we really were going to talk, because we promised not to do any kissing. But something happened that broke that spell, and it wasn't me!

As we were talking, I asked Vicki to rub my shoulders. No sooner was my back feeling better from being rubbed when out of the clear blue, Vicki starts to whisper in my neck. This always sends shivers down my back and she knows this by now. As I said stop it, I bend my shoulder to cover my neck on the side she is talking on. Then this girl, who made me promise not to kiss her until after Christmas, places a real live, true blue kiss on my left cheek!

I was so happy that I was allowed to go home with Jim and his father, instead of staying all alone in the dorm. I really liked Jim's dad, but he was an adventurous driver and their VW had no heat, but after dinner with Jim's family and playing games together, I was thoroughly warm and contented.

Jim and I got to have some alone time and we began to talk. I realized that Jim would only let me get so close to him and then he would back away. He said he had sore shoulders so I rubbed his back while we were talking. I couldn't hear what he said sometimes, so I would talk closer to his one ear, and he would turn his head the other way, so I would talk closer to his other ear. All of a sudden I realized that he was turning his head back and forth because he wanted to kiss me, but he was keeping true to our promise and there was still one month to go. I thought that was so sweet and he looked so cute that I quickly gave him a quick peck on his cheek. He was stunned and turned around and looked straight into my eyes.

"I'm so sorry, I mean I really didn't mean to...well I really wanted to do that!" I finally admitted it. There it was! I had broken the promise that I wanted Jim to make. He must think I'm awful, I thought to myself.

Jim smirked and then said triumphantly, "Just couldn't wait until Christmas could ya."

I couldn't believe it. But I didn't complain either. The joy of a kiss! The warmth, excitement and thrill of a kiss! It stirs up the emotions like nothing else. Only God could create a kiss. I laughed and then told her that she, not I broke our promise.

"Just couldn't wait till Christmas, could ya."

She smiled and asked me if I was angry. Ha! No way was I angry. I got up and asked her if she wanted a drink of water. I got some water and then came back to take my turn in breaking the promise. We kissed that night and talked some in between, the promise was gone, but it was worth the wait.

Her parents came Thanksgiving Day and we didn't see each other until Sunday night at church. For some reason, Vicki seemed nervous when we finally saw each other in the lobby before the evening service. I think she was afraid that after we kissed, I would want to end our relationship. Perhaps that was all I wanted in the relationship after all, she thought.

I assured her that was not the case and told her that I still enjoyed being with her and that if anything, the kiss made me feel closer to her. I know it was only a feeling, but I liked it.

She also told me that she was afraid I might not be a good kisser. She said that she wasn't worried anymore. What a profitable Thanksgiving break it was!

We had entered the realm of the physical. It was bound to happen, but now we needed to guard our passions. Too much would blind our ability to judge whether we were strengthening other areas that were needed to keep this relationship strong.

"Above all else, guard your affections.
For they influence everything else in your life"
Proverbs 4:24 LB

Chapter 10

Falling In Love

〰

Love is such a diversified word. We say we love sports, we love pizza and we love another human being. The Greek language has different words they use to express love. There is the physical kind, (eros), the family kind (philea), the friendship kind (storge), and the committed and unselfish kind (agape.) It is this last type of love that is long lasting. It is this love that can handle the storms of a relationship. This love is a foundation for a great relationship. It thinks more of the other person than of yourself. It wants to give more than receive. It is thinking that you are ready to make an unconditional commitment to an imperfect person. It is more than a feeling, it is a choice we make.

Christmas is a great time of year and a fun time to be falling in love. The lights of the city, the soft snow and the wonderful music added beautiful romance to us as if we were living out a movie. We had decided to get one gift for each other. This took some thought. It all began on one of Jim's and my dates. In the middle of cold December we went out to eat at an ice cream parlor. As we were there, I asked Jim if could see his wallet as we were waiting for our order to come. I just wanted to look at his pictures. He sheepishly brought out his wallet and almost apologetically handed it to me. When I opened it up, I realized why he reacted this way, because there in the "first" place in his wallet ...the first picture that everyone sees when they first open your wallet was a picture of ANOTHER GIRL! This girl looked very familiar to me, because in the last few weeks she had come up to my room a couple times and here was her picture in his wallet!

"Who is this?" I asked

"It's my old girlfriend," he replied, "I just never took the time to take it out."

"Oh" was about all I could get out.

I decided there and then that this man needed a new wallet, new pictures and all!

I think he liked his Christmas wallet, full of pictures of ME with a few spaces left for pictures of his family...and no "old girlfriend" picture at all!

With the coming of Christmas break, I was not looking forward to the school break as much as I did in previous years, primarily because I would be separated from Vicki. Our relationship was flourishing, and I didn't want anything to destroy it. I guess we would find out if many miles did indeed make the heart grow fonder. She would be going to Florida for the Christmas break with her family and I would travel with my family to Rochester, New York to visit my family.

Before we left for our break, we wanted to exchange some Christmas gifts. I tried to think of something appropriate to give to Vicki. I needed to give something that showed her that I really liked her, but something that was not so costly or overbearing. After all, our relationship was still new. We still didn't know if this was love or not. As I wandered through the department stores in downtown Chicago, I couldn't quite come up with the perfect gift. We were only going to give one gift, but what could show her my growing adoration and yet stay simple. I finally found what I was looking for. It was simple, cuddly, sweet, innocent and not so expensive. A Teddy Bear!!

Vicki sent a nice sweet message with her gift. It also was simple, inexpensive and something I could keep close to me. It was a new wallet with her picture in it and no one else's! I got the message!

My family and I and a girlfriend traveled to Florida for Christmas break. My grandparents had retired there and a couple of college girls were excited to relax, sleep, and get a tan! I talked about Jim and clung to my new Teddy Bear named "Smitty" (after Jim Smith who had given me this Christmas present). I talked about Jim almost all the time.

One day my mother finally declared, "Is that all you can talk about Vicki?"

I hadn't realized that I had talked about him so much until she said this, so I tried to talk about other things, but I realized he was always on my mind and in my heart no matter what I was doing or who I was with. I was thrilled beyond words when I received three letters from him at our motel in Florida. I hoped he was as excited about my letters. His letters sounded like he was having fun, but was also missing me too.

I thought about Jim's character and the qualities I liked about him. As I thought over this I realized that he fulfilled ALL my required traits on my list for a husband and all except one on my desirable list. This could be the man I marry. This was an exciting, yet scary moment realizing that I was only 18 1/2, yet I had been praying for these qualities since I was 15, for 3 years and I really had a perfect peace about this relationship.

In fact one day Melanie, my girl friend and I were walking down the road in Florida and two college guys kept getting closer and closer to us, kicking little stones our way. We knew they were trying to get our attention, perhaps flirt a little, but we were getting a little scarred and a lot annoyed.

"Hey, you guys stop it," I blurted out, "I'm practically engaged!"

It did the trick. The guys walked the other way and we kept on walking. The whole time I'm thinking what did I say? Why did I say I was practically engaged? When we were far enough away, Melanie asked if what I said was true.

"No. Jim and I have NEVER talked about marriage, but he is the KIND of man I would like to marry." There, now I had clearly said it and said it ALOUD!

Coming home was very exciting because I was soon to see Jim. We were going to his Men's Choir Concert and then Jim and his roommate were going to stay overnight at our home and then leave again the next day. I was just so excited to just even see him again! I was tan, my hair lighter and I put on my new Christmas sweater. I was ready. When the choir marched in, I saw Jim and he looked very handsome in his tuxedo. Now, I just couldn't wait to talk to him? Our eyes kept meeting through the whole concert. I think he was just about as excited as was.

With so many miles between us and no phone calls at all, I was left with simply writing letters and thinking about Vicki. I really did like her, and the time away from her even made me want to be with her more than ever

As time went on, I found that every moment left unscheduled, every closed eyelid and every passing dream was filled with her. I wrote several letters to her, and I even allowed my relatives to give their friendly teasing to my growing attachment to this girl from Moody.

Soon after Christmas, those of us in Men's Choir had to return to Moody early so we could spend some time practicing and then go on our winter tour. Normally I didn't especially like going back to school early, but this year things were different. On this tour we would stop in Peoria, Illinois, which was close to Vicki's home town of Morton. Vicki and her folks would be at that concert and to make matters even better, Vicki's folks had signed up to house my roommate and me for the evening.

It took little time for me to notice Vicki and her family in the crowd that night. Their tan Florida faces stood out like spotlights in the winter crowd that night. Our conductor was a stickler about keeping our eyes on him while we were singing, but whenever I could, I let my eyes wander to make eye contact with Vicki. She sure was a sight for sore eyes, but I wondered if she had missed me as much as I did her.

Rick, my roommate and I had met Vicki's folks before, and they were all excited to see us both again. Rick had realized that I liked Vicki and now he no romantic thoughts toward her at all. In fact, he was my best encourager. The minute I saw Vicki, I could tell she indeed missed me as much as I had missed her. Her eyes just beamed with excitement and I was pretty sure it was because of me. As she sat next to me in the car and constantly squeezed my hand, I was sure that she had missed me like I had missed her.

We sat and talked with her parents for quite some time, and then Rick and Vicki and I sat and talked for awhile. Finally, Rick said goodnight and Vicki and I were alone in a house full of sleeping people.

The next day on the bus, I couldn't keep my eyes open. I slept the entire time on the bus, finding out only later that Rick had kept the "hound dogs" from constantly waking me up and asking me about my time at the Sutter's. What a good friend!

Coming back for my second semester at Moody was exciting. We really had so much fun together. Jim was so creative and caring. I always felt very special to him. He also took on the leadership role in our relationship. He believed it would be a good time for us to start meeting for devotions together and start developing our personal spiritual lives together. We were surrounded by Bible teaching, great teachers and preachers but we needed to meet together to read God's word and pray. Sometimes, as a couple, this is difficult to do because at first it feels rather uncomfortable. I think this is because your spiritual life with the Lord is very personal, and to share that intimate relationship truly opens you up to another person. It also could be difficult, if you don't really have a true and good relationship with Christ, because you can only "fake" this so long. Even if is uncomfortable at first, couples need to study the word together, and I respected Jim for leading us to this place. We really had fun memorizing the book of "James" together and learning to pray together.

The other creative part of Jim was how he would tell me he felt about me. He didn't want to use the words "I love you" loosely as many do. I knew that if he ever told me this, he was serious and had given this a lot of thought. I respected him again so much for this. However, he used many other words to express his affections for me and how these feelings were growing. He was definitely falling deeper and deeper in love and was right behind him.

As the next semester started, our relationship began to bloom. We would talk on the phone long into the night. I would actually take my phone out of our room, across the hall and talk in the storage room, so my roommate, Steve, could go to sleep.

We decided to meet every night in the lounge and start having devotions together. This not only forced us to read God's Word, but it also was another reason to be together in a positive way. We decided to memorize the book of James. Each night we would read a verse and then try to memorize that verse as well as the previous night's verses. After a while, the process became rather difficult, but worthwhile. That semester, as we sat in Culbertson Hall, we had memorized two and a half chapters of James.

As our relationship became more open, we would go to Moody Memorial Church and sit with a number of my friends from high school as well as from Moody Bible Institute. My father was one of the assistant pastors at Moody Church, so my home church was only one mile from school, so I didn't feel that far away from my roots, even though we lived in the suburbs, 25 miles away.

On one particular Sunday evening, I was making fun of one of my brother's high school friends. He was sitting in front of us with the girls he liked, and every so often would turn toward us and smile. We would mouth the words of a then popular song, "I believe, I believe, I'm falling in love." Vicki then leaned over and asked what was so funny. I told her what I said. Then she looked at me and just gave me that shy glowing smile that says you just said something unexpected, but surprisingly pleasing. I then realized, that Vicki thought I was telling my friends that I was falling in love. This was a very interesting situation! As I thought about it, since it was true, I really didn't mind. that she would think that. Even though at first I was talking about my brother's friend, it came back to me, and I let it stay there.

Being at Moody, we would often look for opportunities to get away and see life together outside the school walls. Fortunately, once in a while, my folks needed some baby-sitters for the evening, and we were more than willing to help. Even for free.

One particular evening, February 1st, we were at my home and talking about something. This was the night that I had determined to tell Vicki that I sincerely loved her. The night in church was just a beginning. I really did care for Vicki. I had often read and heard people say, not to use the word "LOVE" so easily in a relationship. I listened to that advice and would often tell Vicki that I was "falling". That's it.! Just falling. Then, I would say that I had hit the bottom of the well and was digging myself into a "hole" and the hole was getting deeper! Someone once said, "Love is an unconditional commitment to an imperfect person". Well, I was ready to tell Vicki that I cared for her unconditionally.

Perfectly planned events don't always go as planned. I'm not sure when I wanted to tell her I loved her, but the moment I chose was not romantic at all. In fact, we had just had an argument and I left the room we were in and stood by a window looking out. Yes, I still did love this girl, but we wouldn't always agree on everything. Did I still want to tell her I loved her? Yes, but when? The moment was tense and the air was thick with different opinions. But love sees through the good and the bad, and love was still there in the middle of this argument.

I don't even know what we argued about that night, but I do remember I finally told Vicki that this wasn't how I had planned for this night to go. Soon, we would have to be on a train back to school and I still hadn't done what I wanted to do.

"What did you want to do?" Vicki asked.

"To tell you that I love you."

With softening eyes, she said , "This isn't the best time to tell me." "I know, but I wanted to tell you tonight, and no matter what we were arguing about, it doesn't change the way I feel about you. I really do love you."

Vicki smiled and hugged me, and told me something that I would never forget. She said, "I love you too!"

Some people would say that this would be the wrong time to declare your love. But, as I said before, "I knew Jim had given this much thought". When he could tell me this in the middle of an argument, it was a true declaration. His words were not merely careless, but words of a true, unconditional, giving, God-given love that would last for a lifetime.

We stepped into a new arena of our relationship.
We were willing to say that we wanted to care more
for the other person than ourselves. These words
were not easily spoken. We were committed.
Would it be life-long? We didn't know. Even though
averages say that a person will have several true
love relationships before marriage, we were willing
to consider that possibility. We were willing
to practice truly loving one another.

"Love is patient and kind.
Love is not jealous or boastful or proud or rude.
Love does not demand its own way.
Love is not irritable, and it keeps no record of when
it has been wronged. It is never glad about injustice
but rejoices whenever the truth wins out.
Love never gives up, never loses faith, is always
hopeful, and endures through every circumstance.
Love will last forever."
1 Corinthians 13:4-8

Chapter 11

"Special Friends"

〰

Thinking about marriage too soon is not good. Becoming close friends is a better idea. Thinking about marriage too quickly may blind you to not seeing the weaknesses of each other. Over time, friends sharpen one other, and stay committed to each other, see the real person through thick and thin, and even stay close, though they are miles apart. You can truly see how committed to one another you are by how you act while you are away from each other. There certainly are people and opportunities to make us forget the ones we once said we loved. If the heart grows fonder of someone far away, and you remain faithful to that person, the relationship may just be strong enough to endure the coming stressful situations that marriage will bring. True commitment can be clearly seen when the other part of your relationship is nowhere to be seen.

Part of being in a relationship is being in control of yourself and your feelings. Because love is a choice, whether that person is next to your side or on the other part of the world, you must continue to choose to be faithful and loving.. Respect for the other person and your rela-

tionship is required when you are far apart. Here's our first time apart:

As the warmth of spring started to thaw out the cold of a Chicago winter, the budding of tree leaves and greening of the grass gave us hope that a summer vacation was soon around the corner. Our relationship also started to bud and grow as the days together turned into weeks and then into months. We would take advantage of the warm weather and go for walks along Lake Michigan, downtown or some of the nearby parks. I still enjoyed an inexpensive date, and the weather was giving us more options.

Not only did we continue to date more and more, we also started eating more meals together. Usually supper provided the best meal to eat together, and so if it would fit into our work schedule or music group practice, we would eat together. Sometimes we ate alone and sometimes with each other's friends. Each of us had a different circle of friends, but they all approved of us together and we had fun with both sets of friends.

One particular evening, while we were eating alone near the back of the dining room, Vicki asked me if I ever thought of marriage. I didn't think she was talking about us in particular, but about marriage in general, and I rarely thought much about it. I hoped I would get married some day, and from what I knew of her, Vicki would make a pretty good wife, but I really didn't know her that well. Not yet anyway. And I really didn't want to think about it, so I never really did think about it. And our relationship was not to the point of talking much about it.

In fact, I often thought that couples talk too much about the future, marriage and all, and forget to enjoy the present. I have seen too many friends talk about marriage and then soon break up. Enjoy the time now that we have together and let's not get so caught in the idea of marriage and soon they aren't growing closer to each other, but closer to a wedding plan. After the wedding, they aren't sure who this person is that they married.

All this went through my head in about two seconds but my simple response to Vicki's simple question was "No." No explanations or lectures. Just no. She smiled weakly and we went on with our meal. Discussion over. Well, maybe one more comment and I continued to let her know that our relationship was not yet ready to talk about marriage and we shouldn't let other people pressure us into it. I knew that Vicki was seeing a lot of girls on her floor get engaged (it happens every spring at Moody) and that many of her friends thought it could happen to her too. I just wanted to enjoy our "dating" each other right now.

At the time that I went to MBI, there were many fun traditions that the girls had in their dorm. At times "floor meetings" were called so that our R.A. (resident advisor, whom was a girl student who lived on our dormitory floor and was in charge of our floor) would inform us of rules or some activities that were approaching. At these floor meetings we would sometimes have a "ring ceremony".

All of the girls on the floor wanted to be there for this meeting which was usually about 9 or 10 p.m. We wanted to find out who just recently got engaged. The "ring ceremony" would proceed as this: The R.A. would put an engagement ring on a rose and pass the rose around the circle of girls once and we would all "ooh" and "ah" and be able to see it, not touch it. The second time the rose was passed along, whomever the ring belonged to, that girl would take it from the rose and place it on her finger. Everyone would clap and cheer. The engaged girl would then tell us her engagement story, how her fiancée asked her to marry him and then if they had set a wedding date or future plans. We would then have a time of prayer for the couple and then all the girls

who could, would stuff the elevator and the engaged girl would sit at a chair in the front. She would be holding her rose and a picture of her fiancée with her hand ready to show her ring. The elevator door would open and, someone would be holding the "open" button to keep it open. All of the girls, stuffed around the engaged girl, would start singing at the top of their lungs,
    "She's getting married in the morning'
    Ding dong the bells are gonna chime
    Roll out the barrels,
    So get her to the church on time!"

    The girls would sing this over and over to announce that our elevator was on this floor. Then all the girls would come running from their rooms to see who was newly engaged, see the ring and congratulate her. It was a fun tradition and we all loved it. These meetings would be posted on the bulletin board by the elevators. That way everyone would have a couple days notice so they could be there at the meeting. Whenever "ring ceremonies" were posted, many girls would guess that it was me and that Jim and I had recently got engaged. Some of my friends were getting engaged and it was fun that girls thought I would be the new fiancée, however, I also knew that Jim and I had never even discussed the word "marriage". Now I had thought about it ever since Christmas break, and after Jim told me he loved me in February, I knew we were serious. Yet it had been a couple months since then and I really thought we could get married. I realized , I really didn't know what Jim thought about this and I wondered why we never talked about it. Maybe I was more serious about him than he was for me. Even other girls thought our relationship was headed that way. Every once in a while I'd hear some guys tease Jim about being "hooked for life", but he never responded. In fact when anyone said anything about marriage, Jim just acted as if they hadn't said anything like that. He did seem to still be very interested in only me, just no words at all about marriage. I needed to know his thinking about this, so I could understand where our relationship stood in his eyes. I would ask him tonight at supper if I had a chance...actually I would have to take a chance and bring it up.

I was very nervous. This was a hard subject for a girl to bring up. I couldn't sound too interested, but there really wasn't any way to ask this question smoothly. My stomach was churning, so if I was going to enjoy diner at all, I must blurt out these words.

"Do you ever think about (a long pause that seemed forever to me, big breath and then) MARRIAGE?"

There I said it...now it was in his hands.

"No" was his reply.

Nothing else. No explanation. No more discussion. He kept on eating dinner as if nothing had changed, however in that simple word of no, my heart completely sank!

He didn't even have to think about it. Then he added one more comment.

"I don't think our relationship is ready to talk about this right now. We are enjoying being with one another and we need to just enjoy this stage. We can't let other people pressure us into talking about something we're not ready for yet. "

That sounded correct and then it even got a little better...

"You are obviously the kind of girl I would marry someday and right now I only want to date you."

Okay, I think I could understand him a little more. Later I'd have to give this more thought. Perhaps I needed to be a little more cautious with my feelings, because I felt we were ready to talk about marriage.. This caused a few questions in my mind, but not enough to discourage me. After all, right now his eyes and heart were only for me.

Spring Tour was soon upon us, and now that Vicki and I would be apart from each other for two weeks, we promised to write to each other every day. We really did spend a great deal of time talking to each other on the phone each night, and now our time to talk would only be through the mail.

While on tour, our mail call was a great time of joking and comparing whose girlfriend would write the most. I won! Vicki nearly wrote to me every day. This would require her to get a copy of our tour schedule. Then, to guarantee I would receive her letter, she had to write to the churches several days before we arrived.

I would often read her letter immediately, then again before I would go to sleep, and sometimes the next day. I would try to guess what she was writing in between the lines and perhaps where she was when she wrote each letter.

On one stop in Colorado, I got a letter and I waited to read it later that night. On this night my tour roommate and I were told that our hostess would have to drop us off at the church an hour and a half earlier than the rest of the group. So I decided, that since the church was located near the Garden of the Gods, I would hike up a small hill and read Vicki's letter there to help the time pass away quickly. I kept from reading the letter that night, so I could to look forward to it that next morning.

The next morning, with her letter in my back pocket, I arrived on top of this small hill. I could see the church down one side of the hill, and off in the distance I could see the Garden of the Gods. What a great place to read a letter! Especially a letter from someone so special to me.

I found a place to sit down and relax while I cherished this letter. I opened it up and could tell that it was a card. Cards are nice, but not as nice as personal letters. Perhaps something would be on the inside. Or, maybe it was one of those silly, yet "mushy" cards. Maybe even a lock of her hair would fall out of it.

I opened it and there was nothing on the outside of the card except a picture of something. I don't even remember. But I do remember the entire contents of the inside of the card. It simply said, "You are my special friend." She signed it. That's it. To personalize it she had taken the time to underline the word, "SPECIAL". I was on top of this hill for the next hour and a half to read and meditate and read between the lines of my girlfriend's letter, and all the card said was this! Not much to read between or to meditate on. Just a simple underlined friend.

I opened the card to see if she wrote a long letter on the inside of the card. Nothing.! Nothing. She had written long letters before. Some were diaries, some were romantic and some were like a travel book, but on this day, when I had the most time to read and enjoy her letter, I got the shortest letter (card) of my life from her. I read it for an hour and then walked back to the church. I was her "special" friend.

Jim was going to be leaving on Spring tour and I thought he would like letters from me, so I got his choir's schedule and started writing him and mailing him a letter every day to every church where they would singing.. I was excited that he would feel special and receive a letter at every church. This meant I would eat supper with him and then go to my room and write a letter for the next week. He didn't know I was doing this. Now it's hard to keep writing when you're not seeing the person all the time. It is hard to think of new things to say, or talk about, because you have just talked to that person, so I bought a few cards to send to him in between some of the letters. One day I was in a real hurry and the two previous days I had written him "journals", so I found this cute card that said, "You're my SPECIAL friend." Since we had started out as "best friends" and now he really was my "special friend"I thought this was such great card . I was really enjoying where our relationship stood. Little

did I know how that little card and saying "Special Friends"
would forever symbolize our relationship to this day.
We are always calling each other our "Special Friend",
but we know we are "FRIENDS FOREVER"

Friends are great to have. To develop a great friend,
who also happens to be in a romantic relationship
with you is worth your weight in gold.
Developing a friendship should be the first
part of any future marriage possibilities.

" A friend loves at all times,
and a brother is born for adversity."
Proverbs 17:17

"A man of many companions may come to ruin,
but there is a friend who sticks closer than a
brother." Proverbs 18:24

"Wounds from a friend can be trusted,
but an enemy multiplies kisses".
Proverbs 27:6

Chapter 12

"Let's See Others"

∼

If you are truly and honestly happy with what you have, most people will not be interested in looking elsewhere. Satisfaction is in the eyes of the beholder. If someone enjoys their relationship, why look anywhere else? If you like what you see, go after it, and keep it. Doubts may creep into a relationship that perhaps this is not the "right one." Well, there is no "perfect partner." Everyone has flaws. God sets the boundaries in relationships and then lets the individual find someone to choose to spend time or a lifetime together with. Within the boundaries, there are many possibilities. Pray for wisdom. If the relationship is still growing and you see no reason to break up, keep going and keep praying.

Once again, a girl needs to let the guy LEAD the relationship. Many times we grow impatient and we want the guy to move quickly or communicate what they are really feeling. It is good for them to communicate their feelings, however, it should be in their timing and they should not be forced into making a commitment if they are not ready or feel the relationship is not ready. However, the girl always then has the choice as to whether she wants to wait for more commitment or whether she feels he really isn't ever going to make that commitment to her. Patience and prayer are really needed at this time and, as you will see, I didn't quite use enough patience and prayer, but God continued to teach me how to let the guy lead!

The year was coming to an end. It had been the best year of my life. I loved the school where I was,, the new friends I had made, all I had learned about God, and my "special friend", Jim. I was also very excited for what the summer would hold.

During the second semester at Moody, many Christian camps, would send representatives to recruit summer counselors from the Moody students. I knew Jim worked every summer at his church's camp and had been offered the position as Assistant Waterfront Director.. He was praying about whether to do this again and praying about his financial support for a "ministry trip" to the Montreal Olympics for three weeks during the summer. Jim was paying his full way through Moody and always worked hard all semester and summer in order to have the next semester's bill paid. By going to the Olympics, he would miss three weeks of pay, so he thought perhaps he would need to work a secular job instead of a camp job in order to make enough money for his school bill. God would also have to provide for his "ministry trip" to the Olympics in order for him to go. Jim had no extra money so God needed to give Jim wisdom and faith in all his decisions. This was our prayer for him as we memorized James together each night.

I thought of my easy summer, relaxing and trying to find a job in my town. I was the opposite of Jim. I didn't even need the money for college because thankfully, my parents were paying my bill. As I listened to chapels and was praying for Jim, I realized I wanted to do more with my summer. I told the lord I was willing to do something for Him this summer.

My church camp had been instrumental in my spiritual life and I always thought it would be great to be a camp counselor. I knew the youth pastor at Jim's church because as we had already mentioned, I went to church with Jim every Sunday and Wednesday and Jim's dad was on staff with Fred. Fred, the youth pastor was the representative for the church's camp because he was also the Camp Director for the summer program. I went to see him and he gave me an application and encouraged me to apply. I had to pray to make sure that my motive for being a camp counselor was not to just be with Jim for the summer. However, I also knew that Jim may not even take the job at camp this summer, so as we prayed I realized that this would be an opportunity to serve Christ and win kids to Christ or help them to grow. This was an opportunity with "eternal results".

It was around that time that God showed Jim and I that ALL FINANCES are in His hands. Jim made one phone call and received ALL his finances for his trip to Montreal. God had placed on one man's heart to supply the entire cost of the trip. It was a thrilling answer to prayer. Jim then decided he would work the rest of his summer at camp seeing that God had supplied his need for the extra mission's trip, Jim believed that God would also supply the money needed for his Moody bill the next semester. Once again God did supply that extra money. Because it took a lot of work to get the waterfront in order for the summer, Jim would work an extra three weeks before the rest of we counselors would come for counselor training and work also a couple of weeks after we left in order to close it down. Not only did God provide ALL of Jim's ministry support, but also gave him back his three weeks of work that he would have missed plus even more. One can never out give God! It was exciting for us to watch God move and answer our prayers!

As the semester came to an end, Vicki and I often talked about the summer, and what we would be doing. Both of us would be working at Camp Moyoca for awhile and we were excited about that. A summer at camp was something I always enjoyed and this would be my fifth summer at the Camp. I was going to be Assistant Waterfront Director and Vicki was going to be a Counselor. My time at camp began soon after school ended, but Vicki didn't have to report to camp until three weeks after school was out.

The other exciting part about this summer was that I had been accepted to join a group from Moody to go to the summer Olympics in Montreal, Quebec, and help counsel after the showing of their Moody Science films. We would be there for three weeks, and have several opportunities during our free time to see, in person, some of the Olympic games.

I had seen the announcement of this opportunity earlier in the semester and had signed up, just to see if there was a chance I would get accepted. After I was accepted, I found out that I had to raise all my support for this trip. This would be hard for me, since I was putting myself through school, and only had enough money in my account for next semester's school bill. Well, after talking to my folks and Vicki, we prayed for the money, and I set out to raise my support. My dad had given me a list of some people to call that might want to support me, so I called the first name on the list.

God works in marvelous ways, and this stretch of my faith gave me a brief glimpse of how quickly God can work in any situation. That first call, the man at the other end agreed to give me a third of my cost. Then he said, "he would talk to the church mission committee to give me the other two thirds." All done?

He cut me off when I started to tell him about details of the trip and simply said,

"Jim, how much do you need?"

I said, "Just as much as you want to give me."

He replied, "How much is the entire trip?"

God works in mysterious ways. The entire trip in one call! That has never happened to me since then, but I know that if God is in it, it will get accomplished.

So the trip to Montreal would be at the end of July. What a great summer. Camp, Vicki and the Olympics. What could be better?

The school year was finally coming to a close. However, before summer vacation would come, the final exams had to be hurdled. The final term paper, an hour exam on everything we ever studied this semester and several more creative ways to test my ability to recall information waited for me at the end of the semester. The saying goes, it's always darkest at the end of a tunnel, and so it was with school. Exam week was the toughest week of the year for me.

My year with Vicki was also coming to an end. We had really established an honest, loving, sincere relationship that I thoroughly enjoyed, and hoped to see it continue. I felt we had worked through many different situations and still found out that we remained friends and wanted to spend time together. I even found out that Vicki wanted to spend more time with me than I was willing to give.

The only thing that brought me a little confusion was that lingering doubt about whether Jim loved me as much as I loved him. I was still contemplating his answer to my question about marriage. He didn't think we were ready to talk about marriage yet and yet I thought we were ready...in fact I thought it was exactly that time in our relationship. I wondered what the doubts were that Jim had in discussing a future with me. But I promised myself I wasn't going to bring it up again until Jim did. By now, it was exam week, another month had gone by and Jim still had not mentioned or even alluded to marriage.

I liked being with my friends, but I longed to be with Jim more than anyone else. Since I knew we wouldn't be seeing each other for three weeks after exam week, I wanted to spend as much time as possible together. I asked Jim if we could get together for a little time one night. Jim said a bunch of his friends and him were going to be studying ALL night.

I couldn't believe it would be all night, and couldn't he just take a little break and come to the lounge. I could make him some brownies and surprise him. But he said this was an important test and he would be studying all night. Oh well I baked some brownies anyway and my friends and I were having a great time together. We had our window open in our room, since it was a cool evening in May. All of a sudden we heard loud laughter and voices outside and when we looked outside I was shocked to see Jim and his "studying all night" friends joking along on their way to the gym with a basketball. Had he lied to me? Did he just not want to hurt my feelings? Did he really want to be with them more than with me? Couldn't he at least have called me? This made me realize that yes indeed perhaps I loved Jim more than he loved me. I was very hurt and angry. When I knew he had arrived back at his room, I gave him a call and asked how his studying was going.

"Great." he said.

One night during exam week, the guys on my floor were all studying intensely for several exams we had the next day. Vicki had called and asked me if I wanted to get together for awhile, but I declined because many of us were in the same class and we were quizzing one another. This would really help me with the test the next day, so after a short conversation, we said good-bye.

Hours later, our brains needed a short break. We decided to play some basketball for a while, before getting back to studying. I joined in, but never called Vicki to see if she still wanted to get together. I really just wanted to play basketball with the guys and then get back to the books. There are times to maintain other friendships while dating, and this was one time I wanted to be with "the guys".

The problem occurred when Vicki looked out her window just when all of us were heading for the gym, and she saw me, with my friends, and we were obviously not studying. Well, later that night she called and wondered how studying was going. I said we were doing great and then she got angry. Why was I lying to her? Didn't I want to see her? She was sure I wasn't so sure she understood. We talked for a while and called it a night.

I could tell she had a difficult night, but the next evening, after the exams, we had a good talk. She understood that I enjoy my friends and wanted to be with them, but the least I could have done was to have called her. We both agreed that we had assumed the wrong things about each other and agreed to be even more understanding of each other.

I was hurt. He did lie to me. He tried to explain, but I really did not understand. He tried to explain further the next night and even apologized for not calling me, and I was sorry for getting angry. But there was a conflict within myself now. Jim had every right to be with whomever he wanted to be but I really knew now that I needed to slow down my feelings. I needed not to be so serious about our relationship. It obviously didn't matter the same to Jim, so I needed to protect my heart. I thought, maybe it would be good for us during our three weeks apart between school and seeing one another at camp, to feel free to date anyone we wanted. That way we could see how we felt about one another when we reunited . I thought perhaps by going out with some other guys, I wouldn't be so serious with Jim! Now I knew that I could go out with anyone at anytime because Jim had already told me his theory on a dating relationship. He told me that I never belonged to him. I could always make my own decisions to just date him or date others if I felt I wanted to. He would hope that I would only want to invest my time and energy in him, but it was always my decision and vice versa for him. He didn't believe in this "going steady" or belonging to one person...he would say you belong to one another when you marry...that's what God's word says. However, until now we had both chosen to date only one another but now I thought it may be good for us to "agree" to see some other people for these three weeks apart. We would know it was just for this certain time period to "test" our feelings and relationship.

Then one evening, while we were talking out in the plaza, Vicki hit me with this surprising question,

"What would you think about breaking up for a few weeks before we see each other at camp."

What? I thought we had a good thing going here. Why break up? What was she thinking? Well, she said that this would allow us to have the freedom to date other people for awhile maybe, and if we really missed each other, then we would know that we were right for each other, or something like that.

I didn't agree at all. Why break up a good thing ? If we liked each other, why break up for a while. If she wanted to break up, then break up, but then there is no guarantee that we would get back together at camp. Besides, I didn't want to break up. I loved Vicki and I would remain faithful to her even while we were apart. If we still loved each other, then we should not break up just because we would be far apart. If she wanted to break up, then, as tough as it would be for me, we would have to break up because she wanted to, but if she just wanted to do it for awhile and was looking for my approval, then I said no. I don't want to lose her, even for a little while.

She looked at me and smiled. She, thought through all the confusing words I said, understood, and told me she didn't want to lose me either. As we hugged, I wondered why she had ven brought the question up.

When I presented this idea to Jim, his response was a surprise to me, but truly a relief. He said it was a dumb idea. He didn't need to date others to KNOW whether he loved ME! He said I was always free to date anyone I wanted to, but that didn't mean that he would automatically start dating me again at camp. He said that it would hurt him if I wanted to do that, because he didn't want to date anyone but me so why would I want to date others?

I realized now that my picture of how Jim felt about me was wrong. He did love me, he was in the process of choosing me and in the long run, if God wanted us to be together for life, we would both know and have perfect peace. My role was to calm down, get out of the driver's seat and enjoy the ride. God and Jim would "steer" this relationship. What a relief!

Commitment is a valuable part of any relationship.
Not all relationships make it to marriage,
but any relationship should develop
a sense of completion. We should stick with
a commitment until it is finished or end the
relationship if you don't want to stay committed.
Stay the course, run the race, finish the task. Just
don't quit out of annoyance or inconvenience or
rash emotion. Think through all decisions. Some
relationships will not be long, they are short term
opportunities to grow, but still, finish well.

*"Therefore, since we are surrounded by
such a great cloud of witnesses, let us throw
off everything that hinders and the sin
that so easily entangles, and let us run
with perseverance the race marked out for us."*
Hebrews 12:1

*"I have fought the good fight, I have finished
the race, I have kept the faith."*
2 Timothy 4:7

Chapter 13

"Jealousy at Camp"

〜〜

To always be willing to express your true feelings is very important in a relationship. Giving time and attention are constant needs of all. Of course, timing is important, but willingness to be open and honest is essential. If we only think about ourselves and our needs, wanting all the attention and success, we reveal our own immaturity. We must work hard at meeting the needs of others. We must lose that sense of insecurity. Putting aside our needs and meeting the needs of another is an important lesson to learn, and it is a constant lesson throughout life, in different circumstances, that we must continue.

Sometimes when you think about other's needs before yourself, you must try to make the other person feel more secure in your relationship. When you are having the success or attention, you must remember to give back to the other person so they also feel important. It is easier to only want the other person to make all the sacrifices, but both of you must always adjust to meet one another's needs. If you can't do that, adjust your life to the other person's needs. Perhaps you are not ready to keep that relationship. Here's how we learned to adjust….

I loved my time at Camp Moyoca. Each summer I was involved in something different and this summer proved to be no different. I would find myself as one of the Assistant Waterfront Directors, meaning that my primary job at camp, all summer long, would be to drive the ski boat. I loved that summer, especially since Vicki would be there as a counselor to experience what camping was all about and why I loved it so much.

I had been at this camp every summer since my junior high days and had experienced many different aspects of camp life. I had been a camper, then junior counselor, pots and pan dishwasher, senior counselor, counselor-in-training counselor and now involved in the waterfront. This camp required all its counselors to attend a two week counselor training period. This would equip the staff for the summer, but also bind them together as a strong encouraging group. I had been to many of these weeks, and even had taught some of the principles in the past, but this year I would not be required to attend the entire schedule of meetings. I would be part of the support staff that would occasionally meet with the counselors and teach them in the areas we were working in as support staff, but there would be many times in which I would not need to be or invited to be with the counselors.

This was good and bad. Good, because I didn't need to go through the training again, but bad because I would not be with Vicki as often as I would have liked to have be. Staff training was a time to be with other staff members, for once camp started, counselors rarely were allowed to mix with other staff. They were to be with their campers twenty two house a day, with only two hours off each day. I would now have to be a spectator.

It wasn't all bad. I had plenty of time to be with Vicki and we often canoed around the lake, sat and talked near the lake, or just sit with each other during a meal. However, as the training week progressed, it became obvious to me that there were some other guy counselors that took a "liking' to Vicki. She was her usual friendly self, and so when she was with these guys, her friendliness was easily misunderstood as flirtatious. At least, that is how I was interpreting the scene.

There were times as the week progressed, when Vicki would mention how this camp wasn't what she thought it would be. We were not together as much as she thought we would be and she missed me. She did notice other guys and I mentioned that they were perhaps starting to like her. She thought not, but only time would tell.

Camp was going to really be fun! I had to go to a two week counselor training session before the real counseling began. Those two weeks were packed full with Bible studies, training in their camp's philosophy, group dynamics, team building and training in every activity offered at camp. Our schedules were tight. I soon realized I wasn't going to get to spend as much time with Jim as I wanted to. I would see him from afar but that made me miss him more! Meanwhile, the other counselors and I were developing a team atmosphere. This was important for the summer as we would need to know one another and support one another. I wished Jim was a counselor instead of waterfront staff. But that is not how God planned it and I had to remember that He was ultimately in the driver's seat.

Several times during the day I would take a peek at the group and see one guy in particular paying a little too much attention to Vicki. I didn't say much to Vicki about this, because it might seem that I was overly jealous, and perhaps Vicki was indeed beginning to like this guy. After all, she wanted to break up earlier in the summer, so maybe the end was near. I would try to act natural, but more and more, I was feeling a little left out. I remember feeling like I was losing my best friend, my joy and a very big part of my life.

One day, while the counseling staff was practicing tying knots on the playground near the softball field, I stopped to watch for a while. I wish I hadn't. The ropes were tied onto the monkey bars and each counselor was to demonstrate the different kind of knots so they would be able to to teach these skills to their campers later on. There were several who obviously knew the art of typing knots, and they were helping others figure them out. One of the counselors felt he should help Vicki. Standing behind her, he would guide her hands with his hands which meant his arms were also "around" her, demonstrating the proper technique. In my opinion, he would then linger a little too long with his arms casually around Vicki. She didn't seem to mind, or notice the obvious romantic advances of this new found "friend".

The giggles and nudges were too much for me to watch during my brief observation time. I had seen enough. I was losing her, and it wasn't even a fair fight. When I was around, so was he, but he often had uninterrupted time to develop a strong friendship with my girlfriend. You only can get so close to a girl before a guy starts to have romantic feelings and I could sense this guy was getting these feelings.

I couldn't really blame him. Vicki was an extremely friendly girl with good looks and an energetic personality. I fell in love with her and there was no reason someone else wouldn't consider going down the same path I had journeyed. I couldn't demand that Vicki should stay away from him, but I could at least let her know who much I loved her and how much she meant to me. Too often, relationships fall flat because both parties quit romancing the other. We forget how exciting the simple things were and tend to ignore them altogether. Things like holding hands, talking together, winking at each other from a distance, little gifts, and leaving notes in the mailbox. What a great idea! I had come to expect that Vicki would remember all that I used to do and then stay with me because of the past. I would write a note to Vicki and express my love to her.

Well, anything gets old if nothing is added to it to keep it fresh, and just like a cup of coffee, we need some warmth added to our relationship. This particular counselor was providing Vicki with some attention, compliments, listening ears and adoring eyes. I needed to do something. I had become a little lazy in this attention and it was time to step up to bat. So I wrote her this letter:

"My dear Vicki,

For me, today wasn't the best. With the rain today and not seeing you, except for a while, can really be hard. It was. Today you sent me a note and asked if I missed you. Well, I miss you very much. I still like being a lifeguard, but with you on the counseling staff, it is hard. After talking with you last night I realized how hard it is on you. We have fun together, but I want you to know that I still find you very appealing and I am serious about you....I was reading Proverbs 31:30 which reads 'Charm can be deceitful'. Be careful of your feelings. I know you don't think some guys are flirting with you, but from my point- of- view, I think they are, and I'm feeling a little jealous. If you like me, let them know it. You always feel bad about hurting their feelings. Don't. I care about you and love you deeply...I want to be with you as much as possible, so don't say you're trying to get used to being without me....This summer will improve...

Giving you all my love,

Jim"

The letter was a relief for me to express my feelings better than I could verbally, and it really expressed to Vicki how I really felt. It seemed to give her the assurance of my love and the security of my friendship. Things definitely got better. This guy must have gotten the message, for although he continued to be a great counselor and a good team player, he eased away from focusing in on Vicki. He became the outgoing, friendly staff counselor that everyone, including myself, enjoyed having around the entire summer.

For me, the rest of the summer was close to "heaven". Counselor training was over and the kids had arrived. I saw Vicki with her campers at the waterfront and we enjoyed the staff weekends together. Nothing seemed to go wrong and our relationship flourished.

During one of our training sessions in tying knots, I noticed Jim standing and watching us. All of a sudden he just walked away. I realized that a few guys were around me, but Jim should know that was only because I had a hard time tying knots. I knew he was hurt and I felt badly for him. I wanted to follow him and set him straight so he wouldn't feel unimportant. I wanted to tell him that I only cared for him no matter what. But as he walked away alone I knew that I couldn't follow him. I had to finish my session. I wondered if Jim would be angry with me. Sometimes I would get a little too friendly. What had I done?

Instead of anger, Jim was gentle with me. He came up to me and said, "before you say anything read my note". His note was a beautiful acclamation of his love and desire for me. It was an exciting and sweet note. He also asked me to discern boy's motives and detour them. They need to know that they are only friends and that I was only interested in Jim. I was more than happy to do this. It was a good lesson to learn, that when you become loyal to one, you must be discerning of others so as to protect your relationships. Things went much better after that. It was wonderful working together for the Lord. Jim was so great with kids and so patient, loving and helpful to them. They could see Christ's love through him, even though he was "just" on the waterfront. Many of the girls thought he was very handsome and fun. They were right. I was thrilled that he liked me!

Watching from a distance is sometimes a good thing. Seeing what others see in your "better half" can be inspiring. It can also lead to disaster. Thoughtful and gentle response can be beneficial. Don't let your emotions guide you too far. They can blind you into not seeing what others clearly see or they can cause you to do something you will regret later. Be secure in your relationship. If the other one really cares about you, there will be no one who will become more important.

"Do nothing out of selfish ambition or vain conceit, but in humility consider others better than your-selves. Each of you should look not only to your own interests, but also to the interests of others".
Philippians 2: 3 &4

"Nobody should seek his own good, but the good of others."
1 Corinthians 10:24

"For even the Son of Man did not come to be served, but to serve, and to give his life as a ransom for many."
Mark 10:45

Chapter 14

"Montreal Olympics"

⚜

Good relationships should not slow someone down. Life should now be filled with encouragement to each develop into better individuals because of our involvement with each other. Your goal is to make the other person a better person because they had a relationship with you. Let them go, do the unexpected and watch your relationship grow. Spending too much time with only each other can become too smothering or sexually dangerous. If you want to spend the rest of your life together, you will have to develop a trust in each other while you are apart. You may just find out that you want to spend the rest of your life together because you don't like to be apart.

Somewhere, along the course of your relationship, you will see a "choice" you have to make. You actually can have feelings for different people, but you need to choose to whom you want to be committed. It matures you to realize that "love" is more than a fading feeling. It requires faithfulness and truth and restraint....

It was hard to say good-bye to Jim, knowing it would be three weeks until I saw him or would hear him speak. I was also very excited for what God was going to do with Jim and through him on this trip. God had made it known that He wanted Jim on this trip so it would be fun to see what was going to happen!

Going to the Olympics was quite out of the ordinary for me. I was usually the type who enjoyed familiar surroundings. I didn't have many friends going on this trip, mostly just acquaintances. I wasn't quite sure about counseling people, and it was in the middle of something I really enjoyed, camp!! However, I really had a desire to go since God had made it possible for me to get the money collected. I was on my way. Little did I imagine how that the opportunities, lessons and experiences on this trip would change my life.

We left Moody in Chicago and drove all the way to Montreal in a very nice coach bus. I didn't have much to do, so I ended up reading a book I grabbed while packing from home, the condensed version of "Little Women." So when I arrived in Montreal, I had visions of a family of four little women dancing around in my mind.

The one person I related to well, was a guy named Dave and we ended up spending much of our free time together. We would secretly arrange for some of our friend's cots to collapse after they had jumped into them for a night's rest. Sometimes we would sleep outside the dorm in the backyard, because it was so hot in our dorm room. We did that andl one night we were awakened by the police, who checked us to see if we were some kind of escaped criminals or something like that. I'm still not sure what they were looking for and I really thought it was a dream until Dave asked me, "Were there cops walking around us last night.

With all this going on, plus the opportunities to go to some of the Olympic games and witnessing at the showing of the Moody Science Films, I was writing to Vicki everyday with stories of adventure, drama and the supernatural.

Dave and I would often wander around Montreal exploring parks, shops and restaurants. Since we were in a French city, Vicki had told me to try some French restaurants. We thought about doing that, but Dave and I didn't have much spending money, and French restaurants are fairly expensive, so we would often explore the not so fancy, but very filling pizzerias.

One particular day, during our free time, we found an old movie house. The movie of the week was from 1939, "Gone With The Wind". Since neither of us had seen the movie, and since we had seen much of the town, had no Olympic game tickets, and it only cost $1, we decided to see the four hour movie.

This would really be no big deal, except during the movie is when I decided I wanted to marry Vicki. I really did! Scarlet made me realize the importance of appreciating what you have and not being selfish. She really made me angry because she did not make the best of her marriage to a person who really loved her. What a jerk!

I wanted to have a better marriage. I knew I loved Vicki and she loved me, and with God's help and our commitment to His Word, we would be able to make a marriage work. Love is indeed more than a feeling. It is a commitment to be patient, kind, never holding grudges, and all that I Corinthians 13 speaks of. I realized that I wanted to make that commitment to Vicki. I realized that I was ready to make a marriage work much better than Scarlet and Rhett did.

In my last few letters from Montreal, I hinted to Vicki about what I was thinking. I didn't tell her exactly what I meant, but enough to keep her in the right direction. All she knew was that I wanted to have a serious talk with her when I returned.

I was busy counseling Junior girls, but I checked the mail everyday. Whenever I would receive a letter, I would cherish it and it would help me feel closer to Jim. But God wanted me to learn another big lesson during Jim's absence.

It was a common practice towards the end of the 2 week Junior session of camp fort the counselors and campers to pack up and go on "an overnight". We'd go to a campground in Wisconsin and set up camp, tents and all. We would all hike together, swim together, clean, play games and sing songs together around a night time campfire.

On this particular overnight there was a substitute counselor (I think one boy counselor was sick so this guy was new to us and very good looking). He and I got to know one anther well and were together all day having fun with our campers. His girlfriend had just broken up with him and he asked me, "after our have gone to bed in their tents, would I like to come back out to the campfire to talk a little bit". He needed someone to talk to.

At the campfire, he shared his hurt feelings and what God was teaching him. He was very good in his communications skills, and even seemed a little interested in me. In fact, he had been complimenting me all day and telling me how fortunate Jim was to have someone like me. I felt myself respecting him and starting to perhaps have some interest in this guy. We had been exchanging glances all day, the fire was crackling with a beautiful starry night above us and we had just shared some very personal feelings. At the same time as I felt some interest and feelings developing within me, I had signals going in my brain saying, "Stop! What are you doing - you like Jim." The other side of me said "This is a really neat guy...Jim hasn't written in quite a while...maybe you did get too serious with Jim too fast." I felt my affections beginning to waver and so I excused myself a minute, telling that I needed to go check on my girls sleeping in their tent.

As I walked by their tents, having space, being away from temptation produced a place for clearer thinking. I realized I was at a choosing point...a crossroads of decision...if I choose to stay at this campfire with this guy, I was choosing to throw away the relationship Jim and I had established in that year. I would hurt him and destroy our trust and loyalty. Was I willing to do this? No, I chose Jim and our relationship. This choice also had consequences. I needed to go back to that campfire and tell this guy what was happening here so I did. I told him, that he was hurting and was feeling close and vulnerable to me because I was listening to him. I told him that I had some feelings for him of interest and if I stayed there I would be sorry. Even though Jim would never need to know, I respected him and our relationship and I needed to be loyal to him. I really loved only him, so I excused myself and went to bed with my campers in our girl's tent. Later the next day, this guy came up to me and thanked me for being so honest. He said, "he was having feelings for me too, but by what I did had shown him what real love is." I also learned that love is not just a tingly exciting "feeling" but a loyal trustworthy choice and commitment.

A couple of weeks later, as I was counseling my Junior High girls, there was a bunch of letters for me from Jim. To my surprise in many hints, Jim was beginning to write about spending his life with me...this sounded like the first words of marriage! He mentioned that in a few days he would be returning and wanted to have a serious talk with me..

I still remember coming back to camp after being away from Vicki for over three weeks. Distance, had indeed made my heart grow fonder. Between two buildings was a huge sign that read "Welcome Back Jim". The whole camp seemed to gather at the parking lot to meet me. I did not know many of the campers, but it appeared that Vicki and the other staff members, had made this arrival somewhat of a carnival. Of course, the big moment of this carnival would be when we finally got to see each other again, face to face.

I walked toward her cabin and there were campers shouting and giggling, "Here he comes!" Soon the most beautiful girl in the world opened her cabin door and descended the steps into my waiting arms. As the cheers went up from what seemed the entire camp population, I whispered into Vicki's ear, "I love you and never again do I want to be away from you for more than three weeks at a time for the rest of my life!"

Our camp director walked up and gave Vicki the next day off. We went to an amusement park, just to get reacquainted with each other. It was a great day. I hardly remember any rides but I do remember a tight hand clinging to mine and her smiles and sweet laughter with those beautiful shining brown eyes once again!

I always told stories about how I met Jim, our first date, kiss, much of what you've read in this book....Junior High girls loved this and couldn't wait to meet "my guy". The day that Jim was coming home, my campers and I made a huge sign together that said "Welcome Home, Jim!" We hung the sign from one building to the other. It would be the first thing he saw when he arrived at the camp. This took all morning and afternoon so I took my two hour break to take a shower, wash and dry my hair, curl it and just rest. My Junior Counselor took our campers swimming. Jim was supposed to arrive around 6 or 7p.m. so I planned to start freshening up so I would look good and be ready for supper when he arrived.. That was the plan, but because I didn't sleep too well the night before with all the excitement, even though I had my hot rollers it felt good to lie down on my bed.

All of a sudden, I heard this roars of laughter, screams and excitement starting to come down the path towards my cabin. I jumped out of bed, looked out my window and saw

Jim. He was two hours early! Behind him, it seemed like the whole camp was coming to see our reunion. It was like the Pied Piper and all his followers. He looked wonderful. My heart was pumping. I ripped out my curlers, brushed through my hair and ran out of my cabin into Jim's strong arms. We didn't care that the whole camp was standing and cheering. He picked me up and held me closely and turned me around in circles. While all this was going on, he whispered a promise in my ear that was life changing and unforgettable,

"I'll never be away from you for another 3 weeks of my life again."

I wanted him to stop right there and explain exactly what that meant. Is that a marriage proposal or what did he mean, but then I realized we were in front of everyone, so we just looked at each other and smiled while everyone "oohed" and aahed". Just then the director of the camp walked up and gave me the next day off so I could go to Jim's family's home with Jim that night. What a great surprise.

Jim's dad drove us to their home and we had a family dinner together and Jim told us all about his trip. After supper, Jim hurried me into the living room and gave me his journal that he had been writing in for 3 weeks. He told me not to comment on anything but to just read it through. He wanted me to know all his thoughst that he had recorded in the last 3 weeks. So I began to read and read and read. His journal spoke of how he missed me in his life, how I had become very important to him, about his feelings of marriage especially after watching the movie, "Gone With The Wind". Finally in his final entry he spoke of how he wanted to spend the rest of his life with ME. When I finished reading and looked up from reading this final journal, Jim smiled and asked me how I liked his journal. What did he mean by this question? Was this a proposal or what did he mean how did I like it? I loved it! I'd been waiting for this conversation in our relationship and here it was. I told him I really liked his journal very much. He smiled big and said we would talk more about it later. Let's just enjoy being together.

The next day we went to an amusement park together and had lots of fun, enjoying "looking again at each other" . Now we were going to start a new chapter in our lives.

How do you know you should get married?
It feels right, but that shouldn't be the only reason.
It is a lifelong choice and commitment toward
another person. What is it? For us, it was a desire to
continue to encourage, share and struggle through
life together rather than apart. We wanted God to
get glory through our relationship. We had found
someone to grow old together with. We were
committed….to one another and the Lord!

"He who *finds a wife finds what is good and
receives favor from the LORD.*"
Proverbs 18:22

*"Enjoy life with your wife, whom you love, all the
days of this meaningless life that God has given
you under the sun all your meaningless days".
Ecclesiastes 9:9*

*"But since there is so much immorality,
each man should have his own wife,
and each woman her own husband"
I Corinthians 7:2*

Chapter 15

The Storm

∽

Relationships have storms. Working through difficulties makes a relationship stronger, but only if you work through it. Facing the issues and dealing with them are extremely important. Many avoid conflict, some pretend problems don't exist and others get too busy in other things and try to brush the real issues away. That will not help strengthen the relationship. Talking about the issues and working through it in a timely manner should be the number one priority in any relationship.

Jealousy can cause you to do really strange things. It causes you to think about yourself and how you feel, which causes you to come up with false assumptions. These false assumptions cause you to react to your jealousy and not think clearly. This can truly cause a storm in a relationship...however "weathering" through a storm can make your relationship stronger and give you more clarity.

Jim and I were back at our jobs. At the ski and sailing camp, we mainly focused on skiing the first part of the week and then sailing in the later part. Because Jim drove the ski boat, he was very busy this first part of the week. All the high school girls wanted to be the spotters so they could ride in the boat around the lake. They probably didn't mind the tan muscular handsome college guy that drove the boat either. They would giggle and talk to him constantly and I, with the rest of the counselor,s was sitting on the beach watching.

One afternoon, I was very hot and bored; the water looked so inviting. It would just be fun to have something to do rather than watch the girls in the ski boat with Jim. That's when a guy counselor came over to where we girl counselors were sitting and said, "I'm bored and I need to practice my sailing for later on in the week. Anyone want to come with me?" No one answered. Half of them were sleeping.

"Sure, I'll go sailing with you." I heard myself say. And that began the story of the storm!

The last week of camp is a senior high ski and sailing week. I didn't know it but there were still some lingering seeds of jealousy that had started to sprout once again. The storm of jealousy was just about to begin.

The tough job of a waterfront ski instructor was that I had to teach people how to ski all day long. So while Vicki was often on shore, I would be in the boat, often with several girls or guys, going around the lake. I didn't often invite Vicki on the boat because she had to stay with her group of campers on the beach while some of the other campers were learning to ski.

One particular day, I suppose it was Vicki's free time in the afternoon, I noticed that she and this same counselor from the beginning of camp had taken a small sailboat out onto the lake. What was going on? Vicki knew how I felt, and this certainly didn't look good. Here was my girlfriend out in a small sailboat with another guy who hardly knew how to sail. I should know. I had taught the counseling staff how to handle these small sailboats, and this guy, although he knew the basics, was not the expert in the water. If Vicki wanted to go sailing, I would not have minded so much if she went out with someone who knew how to sail fairly well, even if it was another guy. Although if it were another girl counselor, it would have made me feel even better.

Well, the old jealousies started to creep up my spine. I knew Vicki's feelings to me were true, but I didn't want him to start thinking that perhaps Vicki did like him after all. As the skiing continued, I would keep my eye on the small sailboat each time we passed them. Occasionally I would get too close and our wake would cause their sailboat to almost tip. I guess I wanted to show Vicki how incapable this guy was at sailing, and that she should have waited for me to take her. I figured this perhaps was the wrong thing to do, because the next time we passed the sailboat, Vicki gave me that mean look that says "knock it off" and stay away from here.

I didn't want to get her too angry with me, so I steered the boat away from them, while still keeping a watchful eye on them. I also had to keep a watchful eye on the weather, and I had noticed some big thunderheads rising over the horizon. Being out on a sailboat with the wind picking up is not the best place to be, so before the winds picked up I signaled all the boats to come in, including Vicki's friend's boat.

Well, they must have seen the clouds also, for they were already starting to turn back to camp when the worst thing possible to happen to a sailor happened. They flipped. My first reaction was that of anger. I didn't want them swimming near each other and clinging all over each other to "right" the sail boat . So when I reached camp, I sent another counselor to go and help them. The only problem was that I still was teaching ski lessons, and the only other way out to Vicki was to use a rowboat. So I sent this other guy counselor out in a rowboat to rescue Vicki's boat.

This was not working well, since the guy I sent out was little or no help in the situation. He was totally exhausted when he reached their sailboat and the wind started to blow both of them away from camp. Finally, after the ski time was done and just as the winds began to pick up, I took another lifeguard with me and went to rescue Vicki and the sailboat crew. They had already gotten the sailboat righted but they were having trouble sailing and rowing into the wind. Vicki was not a happy camper, and I was still a little upset. I tossed a rope out to the rowboat and told him to tie the rope to the bow and then grab the line and hang on. I then pulled them in just before the storm blew in.

Vicki was not happy, and neither was I. Later that night, we had a bit of a discussion. I perhaps should have handled the situation better. I felt she should not have gone out in the first place. She admitted being a little bored on the beach watching me with everyone in the boat and wanted to have a little fun herself. This one counselor was just in the area. Well, from then on, during the break, if Vicki wanted to go on a ski boat she went with me, and if she wanted to go sailing, I took her, or she waited for me or went with some other girls.

We were sailing along nicely until Jim would make these huge waves with the ski boat. At first it was kind of cute; at least he was giving me attention! But it started to get pretty annoying, when he would make huge waves every time he came around the lake or by us.

I gave him a "Stop it!" look and everything seemed fine until the sun went behind the clouds and the clouds quickly came rolling in, along with strong winds. The worst thing happened then, our sailboat flipped and our mast fell to the bottom of the lake. It took a lot of work to finally turn the sailboat over and the water was cold and the wind was cold. But more than that....where was Jim? I thought that when he saw that I had been capsized, he would drive the boat right over to rescue me...you know, the "damsel is in distress" hero. Especially since the weather was getting worse and he knew a storm was coming. But he just continued to help the "girls" learn to ski. Oh, he did send another counselor in a rowboat to help us. Of course by the time the guy had rowed across the lake against the wind, he was exhausted. I was shivering, tired, scared and upset. As the rain began, and after it seemed as Jim had found everything else he could possibly do, he drove the ski boat to us. He threw us a rope and told us to hold on tight. A couple of times he took off real fast and we couldn't even hold onto the rope. Finally, he went slowly enough for us to hold on. He didn't even say a word like "Are you OK? Sorry I couldn't get here sooner. Would you like some towels to keep warm?" I was really angry. How could he treat someone, especially the one he claimed to love, like this? I figured he was guy counselor, but that was NO reason to put my safety or health at risk! This was wrong!

When we got to the camp, we put the sailboat and row boats and equipment away in the pouring rain without saying a word to each other. I quickly went to the infirmary because I really wasn't feeling well. It turned out to be strep throat, which I had been battling all summer. I took a hot shower and took some medicine and went to bed in the nurse's cabin. About an hour later, Jim came to the infirmary sheepishly with a supper tray for me. We talked out the jealousy. He has nothing to worry about. I have chosen him and want to spend the rest of my life with him and this time he says the same of me. I guess it's good that we still get jealous about each other's attention, yet we can't use that jealousy for hurting one another and not protect one another.

We learned to communicate that summer. We grew to understand and express our feelings to each other in well timed, sincere conversations and always spoke in loving ways. Vicki had thought that being so close to each other that we would see little things we did not like about each other and therefore break up. But the exact opposite happened and we grew to love even the little things about each other. It was sometimes just watching the other one interact with staff members, campers or just watching each other handle life that continued to cement our lives together.

We didn't need to hide from each other. After all, who would want to marry someone that you really didn't know everything about. There are times that people spend a long time together and they do see something they don't like and do break up. In the long run, it is better to break up now than to find that you married someone you don't know. Time is a great healer of wounds and also a great connoisseur of character.

Towards the very end of the summer Vicki and I went to the Illinois State Beach Park on our day off. I remember the day, primarily because I actually started talking to Vicki seriously about marriage and what each one wanted in a spouse. We knew we were talking about each other, but we often would use the third person type language.

Vicki said, "she had always thought that missions was something that God had called her into and she wanted to know if that was something I felt I would be interested in. Honesty in a relationship is important, and I had to be honest with Vicki and tell her that I never thought that missions was something I wanted to do, but that I was open to something full time in Christian work. At the time I was considering Christian Camping as a full time occupation, but if God had other plans, even missions, I was open to it.

Here I was, soon to be a college senior, and I had no sure idea what my occupation would be. My father was a pastor, and many of my friends were going into the youth ministry, but I was still unsure. I knew I loved Vicki and wanted to marry her, but I couldn't promise a definite future, other than I was open to do whatever I felt God wanted me to do. At the time, I felt it was Christian camping. We felt comfortable with our future together, but now both of us felt it would be a good time to let our parents in on our plans.

That weekend, after the storm, we decided to choose the day to start talking about plans to marry. We decided to go together to Illinois State Beach. We had a day off and Jim had the camp van so we took off to have a great day alone!

Jim talked about all the people he had talked to about salvation at Montreal Olympics. As he reviewed it, he thought he saw God working through him with young people. He also saw the influence that Christian camping had on young lives so he believed he would like to be in full time ministry for the Lord, probably in camping. This was important to me as I had on my "absolute requirement" list that my husband needed to want to go into full time ministry. I always perhaps thought full time ministry was missions, but God had opened my eyes and heart that there were many areas of service in full time ministry. We were excited to see how God was bringing our separate lives into one.

But the time for separation had come. I was to go home for about 3 weeks until college started again and Jim would stay at camp to close up the waterfront. He had promised he'd never be away from me for another 3 weeks, so he said he would come down to Morton, my hometow,n for a weekend in the middle of the 3 weeks. Jim said he was probably going to talk to my father that week-end about marrying me. I was very excited!

While I was home for the week before Jim came, I kept bringing up the subject of marriage to my mom and especially my dad to see how his reaction would be. He would ask me why I wanted to marry Jim and perhaps not still date around. I was only 19 years old. So I would tell him of Jim's character of faith and patience. My dad would say I was too young or I still had college to continue and would just shake his head, no. I was a little fearful of Jim wanting to talk with my dad, thinking that my dad may say "no" to him. I wasn't sure if this was the right timing. I was thinking maybe Jim should wait to talk to my dad.

My folks kind of knew what was going on and so did Vicki's folks, but I wanted to follow the traditional approach and ask Vicki's father for his daughter's hand in marriage. I wanted to have his approval since couples indeed enter a family structure and I wanted to be accepted by Vicki's family. People not only marry each other, but also their respective family, along with all the joys and struggles. After our camp finished for the summer and just before school started again, we went down to Vicki's home to ask the big question.

On Saturday, just before I asked her father, Vicki was so excited about what I was about to do, she wanted to go for a walk and make sure I really wanted to go through with asking her father. I assured her I felt it was the right time and then told her that all she had to do was somehow get her mom out of the same room so her father and I could talk for a short time. I would do the rest!

I was very excited to see Jim when he arrived at my house. However, I persuaded him to take a walk with me to a park that was across the street from my house. On our walk, I asked Jim if he still wanted to talk to my dad and I told him about what happened every time I brought up the subject of marriage. I told him of my feelings that perhaps this wasn't the right timing and maybe we should wait. Jim said he still wanted to ask my father's permission to marry me. The only thing he wanted me to do was leave the room with my mother so Jim could be alone with my dad. We prayed together in the park and then went back to my house.

We had a lovely supper and then sat around to watch a preview football game...the Bears were playing and that's my dad and Jim's favorite team. I sat there wondering how to slyly persuade my mom out of the room. What excuse could I use? What was dad going to say to Jim? Would my dad be mad or what? I had to do my part in getting my mom out of the room, so Jim could do his part. Jim looked at me and smiled, so I jumped up and so slyly said, "Come on mom, let's go to my bedroom!"

"Why?"

Now this wasn't an unreasonable question for my mom to ask. She had no idea why out of the clear blue, while we are all together that I would want her to come to my bedroom. Oh no, my bedroom. Why DID I want her to come there? What would be a reasonable answer to that question? Off the top of my head I said, "I want you to come and look at my bedspread!" Now I had the same bedspread that I had for years so I don't know why I said that. I wasn't too clever at this, but my mom came, so at least it did the trick. When my mom arrived in my room, I told her that Jim just wanted to have some time with dad alone, so we could just sit there for awhile and talk. My mom was kind and just sat and talked with me for awhile. I don't know what we talked about.

However, I do know that when mom and I returned to the family room, dad and Jim looked very relaxed and comfortable.

Later, while we were sitting watching a football game, Vicki asked her mom to come back to her room to see her bedspread. I looked at Vicki, hoping she could have come up with a better, less obvious way of getting her father and I together.

Her mom said she had already seen her bedspread, but Vicki persisted that she should come back and see it again. This was the same bedspread that Vicki has had for years, but perhaps thinking it was ripped or something, or thinking maybe Vicki wanted to talk, her mom went with her.

I knew time was short, so I simply asked. It went something like this.

"Mr. Sutter, I really love Vicki,

and with your permission, we would like to get married. I am asking your permission to marry Vicki."

He calmly said that he thought we made a great couple and that usually they went down to Florida for Christmas, but this year they would stay home and he thought that would be a good time to get engaged.

In other words we received his permission to get engaged, but it would have to be around Christmas if I wanted to honor his wish. I did. It would be our secret for the next four months. However, I knew I had received his blessing.

Maybe I hadn't given Jim enough time, or maybe he decided to not ask my dad after all. I had no idea, so when the game was finally over, and Jim and I could go and talk he told me that he simply asked my dad if he could marry me and my dad said, "Sure." I couldn't believe it, after the last 2 weeks of talking and telling Dad why it was a good idea, all he said to Jim was "Sure!" This was amazing. Now what was the difference? I didn't know, but at the same time I knew that "sure" meant "yes" and Jim and I had my father's permission to spend the rest of our lives together!

Working through our storm allowed us to bring our relationship to a new level. Talking about difficulties and misunderstandings are a never ending necessity to keep your relationship growing. You are either growing closer together or farther apart. Relationships never stay still. It takes continual dedication to sail the boat through the calm and storms of life in order to stay afloat. Don't quit talking about the hard issues. We had decided to marry. Marriage really means that you are not only willing to spend the rest of your life with one person, but you are also entering a relationship with their family, whether you want to or not. With that come more storms, and yet, after working through those storms, the benefits are even greater.

"Therefore, if you are offering your gift at the altar and there remember that your brother has something against you, leave your gift there in front of the altar. First go and be reconciled to your brother; then come and offer your gift."
Matthew 5:23,24

"In your anger do not sin:
Do not let the sun go down while you are still angry, and do not give the devil a foothold."
Ephesians 4:26

"Get rid of all bitterness, rage and anger, brawling and slander, along with every form of malice. Be kind and compassionate to one another, forgiving each other, just as in Christ God forgave you".
Ephesians 4:31 &32

Chapter 16

"The Waiting Game"

〜

Waiting is difficult. Waiting for something you want seems like forever. Waiting for something painful, like going to the dentist, can make your stomach turn into knots. It calls for patience and reveals just how patient you are. It is about developing trust, learning to be patient, and finding other things to do that will help make the waiting easier. "Good things come to those who wait", does have some value to it. Someone said "love can always wait to give, lust can not wait to get." Patience is a virtue that comes from developing self control, not being so selfish and allowing others to be in control. Praying for patience is good, but realize that patience will grow through disappointments and broken plans.

Well girls, here we go again. Yes permission had been granted, but once again as a girl, I wanted to control the circumstances and push forward to the next step. I wanted Jim to ask me to marry him the next day or so after we were granted permission. I needed to remember that I am the follower and Jim is the leader. I needed to just enjoy the relationship where we were and trust Jim to lead us to the next step. I just couldn't wait again. Girls, we need to

WAIT for the guy to LEAD. TRUST in him and the LORD! Here's my story of foot in mouth, not waiting…

The semester began. It was very exciting seeing all my friends. I was also very excited about every week-end because now that my father had given the OK, I expected that Jim would be asking anytime. After all, this was his senior year and so we could plan our wedding for next summer or so. I'm sure Jim would want to propose to me in Chicago; it was such a romantic city and there were so many spectacular places for a wonderful backdrop of such an important moment in one's life. Autumn was a beautiful season to propose with first the Indian summer, or as the weeks rolled by, autumn had the colorful leaves and the cool breeze. Every walk, every talk could be it! Two months went by and I didn't get a proposal or even a slight mention of one.

Then came a grand date. Jim said we would go downtown to a jeweler's shop. He knew this jeweler from his church and I knew that other friends of Jim had bought their engagement rings there.

"Now we're just lookin''", he said; but that could be a cover-up. Maybe we were going to buy it right there and he'd propose in the middle of the city of the middle of the store!

The November day's air was crisp and my emotions were stirred. This really could be the day. I needed to look good and remember everything. All the rings were beautiful and I was ecstatic about actually trying on rings and this "marriage" thing becoming more realistic. We were really going to be together for the rest of our lives. Jim and I liked white gold because both of our parents had those kind of rings and the jeweler said it better matched the color of the diamond. Then I saw it, the most beautiful ring…so unique from the rest. It was as if it was made for me. Not gaudy but bigger than the rest of the others I had tried on. It was simple yet elegant, a beautiful shiny "marquee" shape. Of couse, when we looked at the price, it was the most expensive one we had looked at. I didn't want Jim to have to pay that much money so I told him I really liked all the rings we looked at . Jim, and the jeweler just smiled. I think they both knew which one really made my eyes sparkle.

We knew it was coming. I had talked to Vicki's dad and I told her that he approved, but never told her when it would be. I knew it would be bothering her that she had no idea when she would get engaged

At first it didn't bother her because of the excitement of being back at school and walking around Chicago's magnificent mile. I even knew a jeweler, who went to my church, so we stopped in to take a look at some rings. Nothing serious, just looking.

As Vicki tried on various styles and shapes, I noticed that her eyes really sparkled when she tried on one ring in particular. Of course she sparkled the whole time we were in the jewelry shop...what girl wouldn't, but one marquee shaped diamond really made her shine. We left the store without any commitments, and even went to other stores to "just look" at some rings, but I knew very soon, I was going back to put a down payment on a .41 caret, marquee shaped, white gold ring that Vicki really liked. I never told her.

It was a wonderful day and I was very sure, Jim would be popping the question any time now. I was going to soon be engaged to Jim Smith. However, the wait continued and continued. We didn't even talk about getting engaged or of marriage anymore. It was as if the month of August was a figment in my imagination. I was trying so hard to be patient, but impatience won.

I had this "thing" that I wanted to keep the date of our engagement a secret. I wanted to surprise Vicki in a pleasant way. I had heard about a guy who placed the engagement ring in a cookie, while it was still warm, and then gave it to his fiancée to eat. Once she saw the ring, she never finished the cookie. Another guy, during the fall, had wrapped several leaves into the ring and asked his fiancée' to look at the colors of the leaves. As she attempted to grasp the leaves from his hand, only the ring came into her hand. What a great surprise! I wanted to do something like that. Something that would be a great memory. I was only going to do this once in my life, so I wanted the memory to last a lifetime. Something special must accompany my proposal.

I continued to make payments on the ring. All through the fall, every week, I made the long walk to the "loop", to continue to pay for this ring. Any extra time I could get at work, I took the overtime so I could make some extra money.

I quit taking Vicki to jewelry stores. We spent time together but I had to keep this ring thing a secret from her, and she doesn't do well when she thinks there is something going on, or in this case, nothing going on. No more engagement or marriage talks. Although we were planning on getting married, and we were even closer to being engaged, I still didn't want to talk about it much, because we were still only seriously dating. We were not engaged yet.

I had read that 50% of engaged couples break up. Many people had been engaged more than once, and I wanted to wait at least until we were engaged to talk about marriage.

This did not sit well with Vicki. As the fall got closer to winter, she started to get bothered by all this "nothingness". I could tell, but then again I couldn't tell. I was almost done with making the payments. My little payment book was filling up fast. Soon the ring would be mine. Soon I would give it to Vicki.

"Around Christmas, her dad said. "We'll stay home from Florida so you can ask her then." So her dad and I had set the time, but no one else knew.

One day Jim said he had to go somewhere so I asked if we could talk a minute first. He said we could, but he seemed eager to get away. I needed to know what was happening. There was no talk of engagement or marriage, Jim was working long hours, and what was ring shopping all about anyway? I was talking faster and faster, releasing all my anxiety when 'plop'; I felt something drop into my lap. It was a little book, like a band book.

"What's this?" I asked.

"Open it up."

I opened it and saw about 3 payments made on....a ring and the fourth and final payment was due. Jim was working overtime for payments on my ring. He was secretly walking downtown to make these payments and once again I was reminded in a very concrete and dramatic way that Jim was in charge! It was his plan and his play and I just needed to wait.

"Oops." Was my only reply. I needed to muster up and then Jim ran off to make his final payment.

I was left alone on the couch, sorry I hadn't trusted him, but amazed that everything was falling into place and at the right time. Jim was going to ask me to be his wife. By Christmas or Valentine's Day, the wait could be over. I loved him for his leadership and self sacrifice to plan a very special day in our lives. I needed to wait!

As we were talking one evening in the lounge at the girl's dorm, just before I had to go do an errand, which was going down to make another ring payment, Vicki started to seriously inquire if I still loved her. What? We never talk about marriage and she doesn't even know if I still WANT to marry her anymore. What? She guessed that the little talk with her dad really wasn't that special to me. That did it!

I tried to explain. I tried to say that I did indeed love her,andt I always will, but nothing was working. While she was still talking, I reached into my back pocket, grabbed my secret ring payment book, and gently threw it onto her lap.

"What's this?", she asked.

I didn't say anthing. All the months of secretly planning to buy this ring, the extra work to make some extra money, the long solo walks to the store, the constant thinking of Vicki, working around her, dreaming of surprising her, showing that I loved her, was all in that book.

She looked at it and then said nothing but "Oops."

"I do love you," I told her, "and I am always thinking of you. I wanted to surprise you, and I still may, but you have to wait. Don't ask so many questions. Just know that I love you, and I always will."

The waiting game was far from over, but it was now a little easier on Vicki, but it was going to be a little bit more difficult for me to surprise her now. I would still do it though!

God is more concerned about your dating life than you are. He wants you to have the desires of your heart and to experience all the joys of life, but without the sorrow and pain that come from going too fast or doing something out of the blessings of God. God does know best, his commands are for our benefit and he will take care of his people. Learning to wait takes courage and strength and self control and a trust and faith and hope in the leadership of the man who is going to lead you through the rest of life!

"Be still before the LORD and wait patiently for him; do not fret when men succeed in their ways, when they carry out their wicked schemes."
Psalms 37:7

"Wait for the LORD; be strong and take heart and wait for the LORD".
Psalms 27:14

"But those who wait on the LORD will find new strength. They will fly high on wings like eagles. They will run and not grow weary. They will walk and not faint".
Isaiah 40:31 NTL

"The end of a matter is better than its beginning, and patience is better than pride".
Ecclesiastes 7:8

"Therefore, as God's chosen people, holy and dearly loved, clothe yourselves with compassion, kindness, humility, gentleness and patience."
Colossians 3:12

"Be patient, then, brothers, until the Lord's coming. See how the farmer waits for the land to yield its valuable crop and how patient he is for the autumn and spring rains. You too, be patient and stand firm, because the Lord's coming is near."
James 5:7 &8

Chapter 17

The Rose

〰

Making a memory is important. Memories are of value. The more good memories you can make in your relationship, the better. They are like mile markers, helping you remember the good times you experienced together. Getting engaged should be a highlight memory that you will always remember with a smile. Make it special, since you will only have one opportunity to make a first impression. Get creative. Make it a pleasant story that you will want to tell others time and time again. Make it romantic, plan it out, be unique. Life gives us a few opportunities to have a good memory, so make the most of it.

A proposal is one of most important and "dreamed of" moments in a girl's life so it is wonderful when it happens and the guy has truly thought about it and planned it "just for her". A girl couldn't feel more loved or wanted when he plans this special moment and then sincerely asks her to spend the rest of his life with him.

The semester was all "wrapped up" and I had stayed at school a couple of days to walk around with Jim and look at the Christmas decorations and lights. It was romantic and maybe this would prove to be the engagement background. But no. My parents came to pick me up and I "almost" knew, or thought I knew that Jim was going to propose to me when he came down to my house for Christmas break. After all, that little book showed he would fulfill making the ring payments by Christmas and what else would he get me. Besides he was acting just a little funny. After we put my bags in my dad's trunk and my parents were climbing into the car, Jim drew me to him for a good-bye kiss. We wouldn't see each other until December 30th. Right after the kiss, I looked him straight in his eyes and declared,

"You're not going to surprise me you know!"

The look of determination charged through his glance as he responded,

"Oh yes I will!"

The challenge was on! It was as if you could hear the theme music of the "Rocky" movie as he prepared for his challenge of boxing. Only Jim was going to prepare for the challenge of surprising me with "the Proposal"!

I can still remember Vicki's last words to me as she said good-bye for the Christmas break.

"You're not going to surprise me you know!"

We had never spent a Christmas together, but I was planning on coming down to her home to celebrate the New Year.. We had not spoken much about the engagement since that memorable December night, but it was always high on the unspoken list of looks, innuendoes and double meaning comments. She had figured it would come on this Christmas vacation. I had hopefully planted a thought that it could be on Valentine's Day, but that was only a wish on my part.

I was planning to propose around New Year's Day, but it had to surprise her. This challenge was indeed going to be a major accomplishment. I had finally purchased the ring and had it in my pocket. I was so excited on the last day at work at a local condo building, I showed the ring to a friend of mine from Moody at work that day!. He was somewhat surprised that I actually was going to ask Vicki to marry me during the Christmas break. This was somewhat encouraging to me that some of the guys on my floor hadn't figured it out I was going to get married. However, I was sure Vicki was expecting something when we would meet.

I had learned many things from Vicki during the 15 months that we had dated and one of those lessons was concerning the meaning of a red rose. She told me that all the different roses had different meanings. A yellow rose symbolizes friendship and a white rose was for purity and commitment. The red rose, I learned, meant "true love".

With this in mind, it was my plan to take the ring out of the box and place it in the middle of the rose petals. I was planning to give the rose to Vicki in order to show her how much I loved her, and after she saw the ring in the rose, I would smile and give it to her.

I was nervous as I drove down to Vicki's home on December 30th to go down on bended knee and ask her to marry me. We were planning to exchange Christmas gifts this very evening. One of my gifts was the engagement ring!

I missed Jim very much during Christmas, but was very excited about his arrival. I hoped he went to work in early so he would get an earlier start for the three hour drive to Morton. I had his three presents wrapped up and under our tree. I was excited for him to open his presents, but his presents to me were much more anticipated! I got ready all day, thinking through how I should look on my "engagement night". I had even bought a new sweater and spent a good amount of time on my hair and makeup. When I looked just as I imagined I should look, I still had time to watch faithfully and restlessly, I must add, out the front window to look for

Jim's headlights to pull in. When Jim finally arrived, right on time, I was practically out in the driveway to meet him before the car engine stopped. He barely walked into the house, and we sat down to open my presents to him that were sitting under the Christmas tree in the front room. He enjoyed them all, and then proclaimed that he would go and hide my presents downstairs in the family room and that I would be able to open them up after supper after he made us a fire in the fireplace downstairs. After all, my mom had prepared this great dinner and wouldn't want it to get cold. Oh yes, I could let the dinner get cold! I could pretty much not care about anything except "one" gift that perhaps Jim was going to present to me. However, I could wait and I didn't want to act too eager or ruin "Jim's surprise"! It really was his move to make, his timing of "the surprise".

Vicki and her mom were never ones to wait to open presents. First things first, and opening presents were always a first. A tradition in my family for birthday presents is to hide presents around the rooms, just to make birthday parties a little more exciting. So when I arrived at Vicki's home, sure enough, they were anxious to have me open my gifts. I however, said I wanted to hide Vicki's presents, so I slipped downstairs into their family room and hid all three of her presents. I then said that we could eat dinner and then have Vicki open her presents.

Following dinner, while her parents cleaned up after dinner, Vicki and I, mainly Vicki, hurried down to open her presents. All was going perfect. I didn't think Vicki would expect a ring during our Christmas gift opening or on the night before New Year's Eve. Her three gifts were hidden in the room, with the rose off in another nearby room, where I would soon retrieve it as a surprise expression of my love.

Vicki's eyes were wide with anticipation, and even a hint of perhaps "this is the night" look, but she never said anything. The first gift was a small tube of lip gloss. It wasn't much, but I didn't have much spending money after buying the ring. The next gift cost me nothing at all, but it still pleased Vicki. It was one of my senior pictures that my folks had bought. She liked it. I could tell she was really excited about the next gift. In fact, she almost found it first, perhaps she did, but waited until the end to open it.

Her eyes glowed and her hands shook as she slid into the couch beside me. Indeed the gift she held in her hand was the actual ring box! As she tore the wrapping paper away, the black velvet ring box appeared. I said nothing, but smiled, knowing that I was about to fool this lovely girl of mine.

Inside the box was a paper handwritten note that said, "I'm sorry I have been so busy. This paper is a certificate for any necklace, bracelet or earrings of your choice that we go and pick out together tomorrow."

It really would have been a great gift, but it wasn't what she expected or wanted. The glow dimmed in her eyes. She politely thanked and hugged me, but I could tell she was totally baffled. It really looked like a ring box. I'm sure she was thinking, "How could it not be a ring,"

Dinner was lovely and tasted wonderful, if I tasted it at all. It just seemed to last FOREVER. I had other important things on my mind, I had waited long enough! We went straight downstairs for the "night of our lives" or so I hoped! My only doubt was that because I had challenged him a couple of weeks earlier, now he would want to wait for Valentine's Day or just "any" day between Christmas and Feb. 14th, so I wouldn't expect it. Oh why did I ever have to challenge him? He probably forgot about the challenge. This HAD to be the night, didn't it?

As I searched around the room, Jim started the fire in our fireplace. I immediately saw the small box which could only have a ring in it. THE ring in it! It was under a chair, but I decided to pretend, not see it, because after opening it, the other two presents would be anti climatic. I needed to help Jim out with his surprise, so I went and found another present first. It was strawberry lip gloss. Very sweet and romantic because he liked my smooth lips and the taste of strawberry when he kissed me. Sweet, romantic and VERY inexpensive (probably because there was ONE VERY EXPENSIVE present awaiting...one more clue to lead me to believe this was the special night.) The second gift was Jim's senior portrait framed for me. Again I really liked this gift, however I knew his parents had paid for the portrait, and the frame again was within a budget for a much BIGGER awaited present, "a ring".

Now I began to get a little nervous. This was the moment I had dreamt of so often, this was the time I had so waited for and anticipated. This was the hour in which two lives were to prepare to be one. My hands were shaking a little as I opened this small box in front of the fire. I had to hand it to Jim, it was a very quiet and romantic spot.

As I lifted the lid, there was no sparkle or moment! There was a rolled up piece of paper. For a moment, I was mixed up, but then I thought, "Oh I get it, it's a scavenger hunt to find "the ring". You know one of those hunts or trails where each note gives you a clue to the next note, until the notes finally lead you to " the prize"! How clever of Jim. Okay...I'll play. I opened the note and read it aloud in a shaky voice,

"Since I've been busy working this break, I didn't have much time to shop, so this is for any necklace, bracelet or earrings that you and I will go shopping for together."

My ears could hardly believe what my mouth was saying. He didn't really write "just" a necklace, bracelet, or earrings did he? My eyes scanned the note again and confirmed my disappointment. My heart sank, my hopes dashed...a nice present, a sweet thought, but not the moment of a lifetime that had been anticipated! What could I say, I

*was so shocked and saddened and yet this wasn't fair to Jim.
I must be appreciative for his thoughtfulness of this gift...
he didn't know that I had expected this to be the BIG night.
I thanked him and said that it would be nice to go shopping
together. Oh man, this means I need to be able to WAIT until
Valentine's Day. Oh well, at least Jim is here with me and
we'll have a good time together, even thought it wasn't how
I would have planned it!*

She recovered quickly though, and we then embraced
and talked about Christmas and caught up on each other's
families. I needed to get the rose into the room and Vicki
out of it for awhile, so I asked for something to drink. Vicki
offered to get us some cocoa to have in front of the fire, and
I wholeheartedly agreed. I quickly ran to the other room, got
the rose in it's vase and hurried back to my seat, placing the
vase on the floor next to the couch, ready to bring it out at
just the right moment. Just then Vicki came running down
the stairs announcing that her parents were coming down to
talk and her mom was bringing down egg nog, one of my
favorite Christmas drinks. It sounded good until I suddenly
realized that her mom would sit directly across from me and
see the rose. She would probably ask about it and then my
perfect plan would fall apart. For a moment I was without
a plan. Totally lost. Then a really ridiculous idea came into
my mind. I told Vicki that I was really thirsty for water, not
egg nog! She frowned and again told me that her mom was
bringing egg nog for all of us in a few minutes. Her mom was
preparing a beautiful tray to bring downstairs, but I told her,
although that was nice, I really wanted some water! Actually
I just really wanted Vicki out of the room so I could get my
plan back in action!

So while we talked, I drank water and dreamed about egg
nog. The conversation with her parents went well, but her dad
must have noticed some nervousness from me, and suddenly

announced that it was time for them to leave us two alone. He never had done that before. He usually fell asleep while Vicki and her mom would talk. This was highly unusual, but greatly appreciated. We were working together, although we hadn't talked much since August regarding the proposal. I stayed true, and he was helping me out. I liked Mr. Sutter very much, but this even made me appreciate him even more.

However, Mrs. Sutter didn't want to leave. She wanted to talk more. So we did, until Mr. Sutter again said it was time to leave. Again, Mrs. Sutter said she wanted to talk, so we continued to talk. By this time I am dying. I'm sure the rose is going to be seen soon. I'm imagining that it's breathing or coughing or something.

Finally, Mr. Sutter stands up and says, "Elaine, it's time to go!"

Oh, "Elaine" is serious stuff. I remember when my dad called me "James" Big time stuff. Mrs. Sutter looked up and then decided that it was indeed time to go..

After talking for a while, Jim said he was thirsty. I told him I'd go upstairs and make us some hot cocoa to have by the fire.

He said,"Good idea", so I ran upstairs.

My mom had a better idea. She knew Jim loved egg nog, so she said she would make hot cocoa for me and bring it and three glasses of egg nog down to the family room on a tray. She thought that Jim and I and my dad and her could enjoy our Christmas drinks around the fire and talk. My mom always enjoyed spending time with Jim also. I thought that was a great idea and got my mind off the disappointment of the "expected ring" and thinking of just having a fun time with Jim and my family during this break.

I came downstairs without anything to drink, but I told Jim of my mom's great idea. I thought he'd be pleased with the "egg nog" idea, but instead he jumped up and said,

"Oh no....I don't want eggnog. I'm really, really thirsty for water. Could you go upstairs and tell your mom I want water instead? Thanks for the idea but I really would like some water."

He practically sounded desperate. Well sure I could do this but it was so strange. as Jim loved egg nog...oh well he knew what he wanted. I ran up to let mom know and we all came downstairs together. My mom, dad and me with the cocoa, two glasses of egg nog and a big glass of ice water for thirsty Jim.

We were having a great time talking together except my dad kept saying that they needed to go back upstairs. It was nice of him to want to give us some privacy, but we were going to be together for a few days. I kept thinking my dad should just relax and that it wasn't very polite of him to act like he wanted to go.

Once again, all of a sudden my dad got up and said,

"Elaine, we need to go upstairs NOW!"

I didn't know what was so vital, but obviously my dad thought it was imperative to leave now and accomplish something upstairs. I guess he figured my mom would stay downstairs and talk to us for hours and then we wouldn't be able to spend some time alone. That was pretty romantic for my dad. He went upstairs, my mom followed with the tray of cups, and once again we were alone, listening to the crackle of a warm fire and enjoying one another's company after being apart for a couple of weeks.

This cozy scene was interrupted when Jim announced that he had one more gift for me. Once again, my pulse began to race and my heart pound...perhaps this WAS going to be a night to remember after all. Obviously, Jim noticed my excitement so he immediately brought me back to earth with the reality of,

"This isn't what you think it is."

*Great. Here we go on the roller coaster of feelings once
again.*

Jim continued, "But I really think you're going to like it."

*Jim got up and gingerly presented a beautiful red rose in
a simple glass vase and placed it on the coffee table in front
of the couch we were sitting on. The beautiful red and orange
glow produced the backdrop for this red rose of winter.*

*He proudly revealed to me, "This is the best way I thought
I could tell you that I love you."*

*He was proud of this remark because he knew I would
be pleased that he had learned from me that the red rose's
meaning was "true love" and he had incorporated this
knowledge in his presentation of this beautiful gift. He also
knew I loved roses and his creativity. Now I hate to say this,
but in the back of my mind came screaming the words,*

*"I could think of a BETTER WAY to tell me you love me...
PROPOSE to me!" but thankfully it stayed in the back of my
mind and didn't find its way to my lips.*

Alone again, I smiled and told Vicki that I had one more
gift for her. Her eyes lit up like a birthday cake, assuming
that it was again the long awaited ring. I quickly told her that
it wasn't what she thought it was, although it really was, but
hidden. I reminded her that she had taught me what a red
rose meant. That it was a symbol of true love.

I got up to get the rose and said that this was the best way
of showing her that I loved her. I was sure she thought there
would have been another way but she listened. As I gave her
the rose, she politely smiled and then placed it on the coffee
table in front of us.

She never saw the ring.

I had no back up plan.

The ring was in the rose but I didn't want to tell her. She
must of seen this confused look on my face, for she immediately picked up the rose and told me how pretty it was and

that she really appreciated the effort and thought that went into getting and bringing her this flower. She was looking back and forth from me to the rose as she said this, but she still was not seeing the ring in the rose!

Then she brought the rose to her face and smelled its fragrance. Of course, Vicki, like most people close their eyes when smelling a flower so as to enjoy the scent better. But you can't SMELL a ring!

Again I must have looked befuddled. What was I going to do? Tell her to look in the rose? Smell it again? Then it happened.

However, I must not have seemed very grateful, because he went on to explain how difficult it was to keep the rose alive and fresh on the cold, icy three hour drive down to Morton. He explained how I had taught him that a red rose meant true love and he looked for the deepest red rose in full bloom. That's when I truly felt guilty. I was so wrapped up in this "engagement" thing. I wasn't really trying to just enjoy the moment and all that Jim was giving to me. I realized my self-centeredness and selfishness and refocused my attention on Jim and how hard he was trying to please me. I decided I needed to encourage him, give him my full attention, and make much more ado about this gift of "true love".

"Do you want to smell it?" he asked excitedly.

"Sure." I replied and took the vase and brought the rose up to my nose, closed my eyes, and enjoyed the wonderful aroma which only a rose produces.

"It smells beautiful." I said turning and looking at Jim.

He seemed stunned or speechless, almost confused by my reaction. I decided that I needed to comment more about the beauty of this flower, so I began to look more intently at it and while complimenting the flower on its smell and beauty — I kept thinking I saw glimmers of light coming out this rose, but then I would think "Oh Vicki, you're just back to wishing the ring is in the rose. You need to get off this engagement thing. It's not going to happen tonight!" Of course I KNEW that would be ridiculous and ONLY hopeful thinking...Jim had already gotten me my three gifts and I wasn't going to embarrass myself or get disappointed again tonight.

Then the firelight would make the rose sparkle again and then I was confused because roses don't sparkle. I tried to unobtrusively bring the rose closer to my eyes so I could have a better look, while inside my head I wanted to tear apart the rose petal by petal, knowing that doing that would only be to my disappointment and embarrassment once again.

I turned to look at Jim and in one moment, the story could be told. His smirk and adoring eyes reveled quickly to my mind and heart that this was it. There was a ring in this rose! My eyes turned to only confirm what was happening. Many girls dream of the guy down on his knee, expressing his long dying love for her and she dreams to share his life with her. The romantic words which she will cherish in her heart forever....words. This kind of tender amazing moment takes a planned speech from a young man and my man had planned every detail well, right down to this moment where with a glimmer in his eye, and a trumpet of victory in his voice, he turned and said the words I would never forget.

"Got ya, didn't I?"

My mind and eyes were still trying to inform and convince my heart that this was really happening to me! The roller coaster ride that my heart and emotions had been on all evening had taken a sudden turn and rise and I couldn't quite get a grasp. I dropped the vase and began to cry. I think it was absolutely tears of relief and joy and being overwhelmed by the moment. My words needed to be just as memorable and the truth was he HAD WON...he had surprised me. So being the good sport that I was, at such a loving and romantic moment as this, there were only a couple of well chosen words to utter.

"You Brat!" and then we began to laugh and then I began to cry..my heart really didn't know what to do.

The firelight must have caught a corner of the ring and for a brief second there came a brilliant flash of light from the rose. I saw it and I know Vicki saw it. A glimmer of hope danced in her eyes, then a cloud of doubt washed it away. She turned to me and I was all smiles. I had done it. She was totally bewildered. She again looked more obviously at the rose, and then she saw it.

That little band of white gold. The shimmering diamond glowing in the firelight. She then knew it was true. Her dreams were about to become reality. Her strength was gone and she nearly dropped the vase! I took the vase and gently set it down, carefully taking the ring into my hand. She was crying and I took her in my arms and gently asked,

"Will you marry me?"

She nodded, not able to speak and then just as assuredly with tears in her eyes, she drew back and sweetly said, "You brat!"

This is what my future bride says to her future groom. These are the first words that come from her mouth after I have proposed to her. But I loved it! I knew she knew I got her. I won. I surprised her! She though she had it all figured out and I did it. I was pleased and she had nothing to really be upset about.

I wasn't finished yet. She had only nodded. I wanted a verbal commitment, so I got down on my knee and again asked her if she would marry me. Through her tear stained eyes came a calm assurance and then...she nodded. I said I couldn't hear her and so with a quivering voice came her promise, "Yes!"

She wanted to rush upstairs and tell her mom, but I said let's keep this to ourselves. Tonight we will be the only ones who know for sure that we are engaged. I also said that marriage wasn't going to be easy. I didn't have a job waiting for me. The money wasn't guaranteed, but if she was willing to go with me through this journey of life, I would love to have her by my side. Only the Lord knows where we are going.

The surprise was a success, but now Jim drew me into his strong arms and told me of his love for me and would I marry him. I shook my head yes, but my sobs wouldn't let me speak.

"You have to answer me this question Vicki." he gently prodded.

Then he fulfilled my dream by kneeling down on one knee, taking the rose and grasping the diamond marquee ring, taking my hand and gently asking once again,

"Will you, Vicki Sutter marry me?"

"Yes."

He placed the ring on my finger and kissed my hand.

In that moment, we had promised to plan a future together. You can't explain these moments. They are as if you stop in time, everything is well with the world. Your heart is at peace like you finally found your way home. We decided to not tell anyone else that night..oh yeah my dad probably suspected, Jim's folks probably thought this might be happening sometime during this break, Jim's friend had an idea as Jim had shown him the ring, but ONLY Jim and I knew FOR SURE. We were the ONLY two in the whole world who knew what we had promised to one another on this night. This was our moment to relish in together and enjoy. This red rose WAS the BEST WAY Jim could tell me he loved me after all!

As God expresses his love to us in many ways,
love can and should be expressed in as many
ways as possible to the one we love. We were now
committed to express our love to each
other for the rest of our lives.

"Show me your unfailing love in wonderful ways.
You save with your strength those who
seek refuge from their enemies."
Psalms 17:7 NLT

"There are three things that will endure—faith,
hope, and love—and the greatest of these is love. "
1 Corinthians 13:13 New Living Translation

Chapter 18

"Best Laid Plans"

❧

Flexibility is a great trait to have in your relationship. Not much seems to always go according to our plans. God's plans are the only ones that always work out. For us, something breaks, someone is late, it comes too soon, they don't understand, or you didn't know, are all common reasons why whatever you planned didn't go according to your calculations. It is good to have a plan, to know what you want to do and where you want to go, but leave room for the unexpected. Allow time to get lost, go a little longer, cut it out all together or just do it differently. Keep the final goal in mind and let the little things stay little. Relax. Don't be so negative. Stay positive and encouraging in spite of the changes and enjoy the ride. There are always good things to be found in new plans. They are just different than what you were planning on.

When making life-long plans, it is wise to receive advice from those who know you and life better than you…that would include your parents, youth minister or workers, teachers, adult friends and the Lord. Sometimes that advice may not be easy to handle. You should always pray about the advice and be humble enough to do it when it truly is

wiser. God sends these wise people into your life to help guide you and they really do usually really love you and want what is best for you. So, just remember to be willing to compromise, listen and don't be bull-headed and keep your eye on the goal...

I had a wonderful night's sleep that night. I was actually engaged to Jim Smith. I would lay on my pillow and put my hand in the air and gaze at my beautiful ring. It fit perfectly, looking to be made just for me just as God had made Jim just for me.

Even though I was sleeping well, I must have been sleeping lightly. The minute my mom tried to quietly enter my bedroom early the next morning, I sat up immediately. I think my mom was just slipping in to get a bit of laundry so I really surprised her. I rarely woke up so easily, but the biggest surprise was about to come. My dad had kept Jim's secret of getting engaged well. I put out my hand in front of my mom's face and exclaimed,

"Look mom...I'm engaged!"

My mom threw herself against my wall and stammered..

"Oh...I'm going to get your father!"

She wasn't angry, just happy and surprised. My dad and mom came back into my bedroom, with my dad telling my mom he knew everything and it was fine. Jim had already asked him for my hand in marriage way beforehand so everything was done properly and with his permission.

My mom loves to celebrate and she immediately began to plan the morning celebration for this great event. Jim was awakened, we got dressed and, took pictures of us together on the first day of our engagement and had a celebration breakfast which consisted of ALL the breakfast food my mom could fix. It was very fun.

The next few days Jim and I just walked around on top of the world, finally free to speak of marriage and our dreams and plans. Speaking of plans, we decided since we were engaged on Dec. 30th of this year, we chose Dec. 30th of next year for our wedding date. It was on a Saturday and I always wanted a Christmas winter wedding. I always loved the tiny white lights, trees, flowers, music and greens of Christmas decor. This would be perfect. I would finish the next semester and then work for half a year while my mom and I made wedding plans. Jim would graduate from Moody and continue at Trinity in order to complete his Bachelor's Degree. It sounded like a great plan. We began to go around to some businesses for me to apply for a job in Morton. Now back to reality and back to college for one more semester but NOW it really would be time for my "engagement" party with the girls on my dorm floor. My ring now would get to be placed in another rose for my dorm party, so actually my ring got to be placed in TWO roses but it was the FIRST ONE that really counted!

When I attended Moody, they had a great tradition recognizing those who had become engaged during their time at school. So after our engagement, I was always fearful that my good friends would suddenly attack me for the traditional flag poling ceremony.

The ceremony was simple enough. Usually after curfew, the guy's friends would take him to the flag pole in the middle of the plaza, tie him to the pole and shout his fiancée's name loudly, over and over. Hundreds of students would rush to their windows to see this poor creature tied to the pole, and try to guess who the lucky couple was. Then the shouting continued until his fiancée came down and kissed him. Kissing, was of course not allowed on campus, and certainly not in public, but the unwritten rules let this one infraction go unpunished. They also unofficially let this happen after curfew.

All this was done in fun, and made a lasting impression on the newly engaged couple. It was actually something I was anticipating with some excitement, but never knowing when it would happen. The frightening part for the guys happens inside the dorm before your friends carry you outside to the flagpole.

Sometimes they would tie guys up and cover them with chocolate and pour marshmallows on him. Other times it was better, or worse. It only depended on your friends. I had good friends, but fun loving friends. All semester I waited. Each night I would wake in my bed, listening for the whispers in the hallway. Would it be after curfew? Would they attack me in my room or somewhere else? Always looking, never knowing. It was almost a spiritual lesson, a reminder of the rapture. Having an idea of what was going to happen, but not ever knowing when.

Our wedding plans were a little bit more concrete, but with a little of the unknown added to heighten the drama. Vicki had always wanted a Christmas wedding. I was to graduate from Moody that spring, and would begin classes at Trinity College in order to complete my Bachelor's Degree. It would take me three semesters to finish up my degree. Vicki and I would work hard that summer and Vicki would continue to work full time for the fall semester in order for us to have that Christmas wedding and be together while I finished up my schooling for one year. We figured we would have enough money to rent an apartment near the school and take care of living expenses and my school bill for the next year.

The down side of this plan was that Vicki would not graduate from Moody. We also were fairly young if we married then, I would be 21 and Vicki would be 20. Although we really thought about this plan, and it was a year away, just a few more months, say in May, and Vicki could graduate from Moody. We wouldn't have to work full time and we both would have one more birthday and more schooling under our belt.

We each prayed about the timing of the wedding and talked with our parents. It's great to see God work because as soon as I started to think we should wait for Vicki to graduate, she had the same thoughts. Our parents also were pleased, and that was very important to us. A few months of waiting now would be rewarded with years of good relationships with our parents. I did agree that for us waiting would be the best but I told Vicki that I would wait for her only one week after she had graduated, so we looked at the calendar and realized that June 3rd would be our wedding date. It was set. I still think between six months and one year is perfect for an engagement time, but we now had a seventeen month waiting time ahead of us.

When we came back to start our classes, we both realized that both sets of parents thought it would be a better idea for us to wait a little longer to get married so I could graduate from Moody and Jim be only one semester away from Trinity graduation by the time we married, instead of a whole year with that financial and emotional burden put upon us. My dad really thought it would be good to finish what I had started. Neither set of parents were against us getting married, nor did we feel as if they would force us to make this decision. We needed to pray and think about this decision together. It's very hard to pray with right motives when you pray about whether you should postpone your wedding date. We really thought our plans sounded good to us and everyone would see that after awhile, but we also decided we should pray about this separately and just think about it ourselves, rather than have long discussions on it together. We decided in fact that we wouldn't talk about our wedding date at all together until we had prayed and thought about it separately. I had determined that I wouldn't bring it up until Jim did. He would be the leader of our relationship, so I would pray and WAIT until his lead of the next stage of talking and praying together about it.

This really was a very good idea because I think we could be more honest with ourselves and more sensitive to God when we prayed alone. About a week or two had passed and I found that I seemed to be more excited about my own graduation from Moody and a Spring Choir Tour to California the next spring. In order for me to graduate or be on that tour, we would need to postpone our wedding. I didn't love Jim any less. I was just still young and desired a few more experiences as a single young woman. But how would I explain my change of heart to Jim without hurting his feelings? How do you tell your fiancée that you want to postpone your wedding date without giving him doubts of your love? I began to pray that the Holy Spirit would guide him in the same decision so neither one of us would be hurt. I just needed to pray, be honest and wait for Jim to decide when we should discuss our decisions after praying about it apart.

About one week after this, Jim decided it was time to talk. We were at his family's home and after dinner, we went into his living room. Jim said after praying and thinking about everything, he felt it would be wiser and best for us to post-pone our wedding. I could hardly believe my ears. This was so exciting. The Holy Spirit had absolutely changed both of our wills and hearts to be unified. God had answered my prayers with a yes. Even though there was great peace with this deci-sion, it was overwhelming to see God through the Holy Spirit lead us to the same decision as we had prayed about it sepa-rately. The power of God and His direct guidance in our lives thrilled me and I started to cry. Jim, thinking I was let down by his decision to postpone our wedding, started reaf-firming me that this would be a good decision. I stopped him midway in his statements and said I agreed with his deci-sion and had decided this decision as well. I explained I was just crying because of being so overwhelmed of how God could completely change our minds. We were excited to see God leading us in this first big decision we needed to make together...we always want Him to lead us this way.

Jim then turned to me and said,

"I'm willing to wait for you to graduate, but I'll only wait one week after that for you."

He went and got a calendar and showed me when I'd graduate the following year and proceeded to count seven days from that date. That is where we came up with our new wedding date: June 3rd!

"That's the date!" said Jim.

Now to many, they would be ecstatic, but I just laughed. Yes, God was asking for me to totally have His will be done, not any of mine. I play the organ, so I have been the organist for many weddings and it always seemed to me (as to many people) that everyone got married in June. I didn't ever want to be a June bride. Notice that our first date was in December, the absolute opposite time of June. However, to me it was as if God were asking me for my complete submission to HIS timing so the answer was,

"Yes, June 3rd it is!"

That night we prayed for our long engagement ahead of us and we claimed the scripture Psalm 118:24, "This is the day (June3rd) that the Lord has made (for us to be united into one); we will rejoice and be glad in it (today we will rejoice as we presently wait for our wedding, the actual day we will rejoice no matter what happens on that day and everyday after June 3rd we'll rejoice that God united us on that day!)."

Little did we know, that we would have to quote this scripture to one another many times during our LONG 17 month engagement!

Besides waiting for our wedding, I was also still waiting for the flag poling to occur. Then it happened. It was final's week. Vicki had finished most of her exams and had gone home for a few days, so I had let my guard down a little. Just a little though, but I still should have suspected something when our next door roommates, Warren and Skip asked me to help them with something. I'm not sure what it was, but it didn't matter. Soon it seemed like the entire floor of guys were on top of me in Warren's room.

They wrapped me in a bed sheet and carried me to the bathroom where they held me down and ceremoniously poured stuff they had been saving all semester all over ME! Maple syrup from the dining room, mustard from the 14th floor lounge that no one ever used, awful smelling cologne, and more junk all topped with feathers donated from someone's pillow...a generous offer to be sure.

After this great ceremony in the bathroom, they headed for the elevator and out to the flagpole with such a commotion, most everyone had reached their window by the time they had me by the pole. Now, since they knew and I knew Vicki was not there, I wasn't sure what would happen. Not to worry, they all started to shout, "Vicki, Vicki, Vicki!"

Of course she wasn't there, but Rick, one of the guys on my dorm floor, placed a mop on top of his head and came out to hug and kiss me. It sure wasn't how it was supposed to end, but never the less, they untied me and I had my moment in the spotlight. Vicki wasn't too pleased that Steve, my roommate, planned my flag poling when she was away, but that was between Steve and Vicki. All I knew was that I took a very long shower that night.

Taking wise advice can be very hard, especially when it means waiting to be married. That is so hard for young people, but when it makes better common sense, the wiser decision needs to be made. Asking help from the Lord and others is wise. Don't rely on your own instincts. Totally trust in the Lord.

"Trust in the Lord with all your heart and lean not into your own understanding"
Proverbs 3:5

Chapter 19

"The Long Wait"

Waiting for something very valuable is hard but well worth the wait. God knew this and so he ordered a man and woman to wait until marriage for them to be unified as one. He knew this would be a great blessing and a great protection to keep one man and one woman unified for life. God will give strength, satisfaction, help with temptation and joy to wait for the great union. God has a great plan in bringing two people together to serve one another and Him and waiting to unify our lives in His timing is to obey Him and wait for His great blessings! This is totally trusting Him and obeying Him, even though it takes self control and patience. It is a long wait but there does come a day when the wait is over and you realize why God planned for the union of two to happen after marriage...for your blessing and protection of your marriage...

That summer I decided I needed to go home and live, instead of work at camp again. I loved working at camp, but this would be my last summer at home and my mom and I needed to make some wedding plans. We needed to make all the wedding plans during this summer even though we wouldn't be getting married until the following summer. I came to this conclusion as I looked at my schedule for the next year, my Senior year at Moody, My Spring California Choir Tour, my graduation and of course the next Saturday our wedding. So Jim and I said our good-byes, although he planned to see me at least every three weeks on the weekends because he had promised that he would never be away from one for another three weeks for the rest of his life. We would also miss each other extremely by every three weeks.

I worked as a Day School counselor with Morton's Park District, but this job was only from 9:00 am to 12:00 PM noon, every Monday through Friday. This gave me plenty of extra time but it didn't take my mom and I very long to make all the plans....flowers, church, caterers, my dress, bridesmaids and dresses, all the arrangements, and when Jim would come down to Morton for the week-ends, we would register for our wedding gifts, picked out the cake, tuxedo's and just have fun.

My mom always says this was the summer where she really realized that my heart was with Jim and I longed to be with him. She said I didn't mope or complain or anything, just seemed alone, so when Jim called by the end of July and asked if he could bring me back with him to camp to work on the waterfront for a week, my parents were quick to give their permission. I was thrilled and my one week turned into 3 weeks of camp work and time with Jim.

Seventeen months was a long time to wait, but we filled it with enough events to keep it from seeming endless. My days at Moody were ended and I could spend my summer up at Camp Moyoca again, since I didn't need to work full time to start saving up for our wedding yet. This year I would be the resident director at camp. Vicki managed to come up for three weeks and help with the life guarding situation near the end of the summer. It was very nice having her back up at camp, as we had missed each other a lot, We did a lot of calling and writing and I drove back and forth from camp to Morton MOST of the summer to keep my 3 week promise!

The next school year started and the absence of Vicki made the days begin to slow down. She was finishing her year at Moody and I was at Trinity College, but living at home which really helped my financial situation. We saw each other only on the weekends when she came to my folk's home. This would have been great, but even then I didn't see much of her because of my crazy work schedule at the local UPS center.

What a great paying job that was, but it was from 10:00 PM until 2:00am or later. I took the job because I needed the money, but I also had a killer schedule at school that started at 8:00 am every morning. So, after work, I would rush home and get a few hours of sleep, wake up in time for class, grab a quick nap in a friend's room in the afternoon before my science lab at 3:00 PM. go home for dinner and homework, before I would jump in the car to get to work on time.

By the time the weekends came around, I usually slept as much as I could, but not as much as I wanted to, since I wanted to see Vicki a little bit. I was usually a "zombie" and I slept that semester away. I still remember the Saturday after Thanksgiving around 7:00 am in the morning I was eating breakfast in the kitchen and my mom came out and asked me why I was up so early. I smiled and told her I just got home, I had loaded trucks all night!

Absence DOES make the heart grow fonder. The next year while Jim was going to Trinity and I was still at Moody, it was very difficult many times. I loved the "hello's" at the beginning of the week-ends, but I hated the "good-byes" at the end. The week-ends flew by and the Smith family graciously opened their home up to me every week-end. We all got to know one another very well. I was thrilled to become a part of this family. Jim worked hard to complete his schooling and his job was from 10 p.m. to 2 a.m. which really meant that he would not get home and to bed until around 4 a.m. , so many week-ends he was very tired. Because he would be sleeping in on Saturday mornings trying to catch up on some needed rest from his weekly schedule, it would give me time with his family to get to know them. In fact our Saturday morning ritual was me making chocolate chip cookies for the family. I think it was pretty nice of Mrs. Smith to have all the ingredients there and ready for me every Saturday morning, and his sisters really liked the cookies. I wanted to see Jim as much as I could so being at his family's house every weekend was so wonderful.

Someday, there wouldn't have to be these "good-byes" all the time! However, being away from each other during the week did help us not to take one another for granted as much and to value the time we had together. We had good phone bills also!

I also saw that during the week I used my time to culti-vate my friendships with my girl friends at Moody.

Being apart also helped us with our physical relation-ship. We were committed to doing things God's way and to obey his principles, even though our flesh would sometimes desire the opposite of His will. We also knew Satan would love to destroy our marriage or any ministry for which the Lord would like to use us by sexual sin. We wanted to present ourselves to one another unblemished and unstained sexu-ally as a whole gift to one another on our wedding day.

As we were apart from one another we would pray that the Holy Spirit would give us power over this temptation and He did. We also realized that we must be wise and not naive, so we made some physical restraints based on I Corinthians 10:13, "No temptation has seized you except what is common to man. And God is faithful; he will not let you be tempted beyond what you can bear. But when you are tempted, he will also provide a way out so that you can stand up under it."

We came up with a good "way out" before it will happen. In January before our June wedding day (that would be 5 months before our wedding), Jim and I decided that until that June 3rd, we could no longer be anywhere ALONE together. We didn't want to have temptation near. This was difficult because your nature in engagement is that you want to be alone. We decided that we had the phone to talk to one another alone or we could take long walks outside together where there were people or sit in a restaurant and talk when we needed some privacy. We were thrilled to watch God help us wait sexually for June 3rd also.

As the spring semester came into view, so did the wedding. I adjusted my school schedule so most of my classes started after lunch and I could actually sit in one place without falling asleep. Vicki took advantage of this and asked me to help list and address all the people we were going to invite to the wedding. Vicki and her mom were going strong on the wedding plans and I even helped a little. I didn't do much, but I did pick out the top of the wedding cake and insisted on the song "Here Comes The Bride" as Vicki came down the aisle. That is all I remember from most weddings and that it was exciting to watch the bride come down the aisle and I wanted to have goose bumps and be excited when my bride came down the aisle to me! That was the extent of my planning for the wedding. I didn't mind. I was planning our honeymoon.

We didn't have much money, but we had enough money to fly to Florida and stay at Vicki's grandparent's mobile home. Of course, they would be up north already, since our wedding was in June, so the two bedroom, two bathroom home with a full kitchen, living room, and the dining room would be all ours for the week, free of charge. This was great, plus they lived only a few miles from Fort Myer's Beach and Sannibel Island, some of the great tourist spots of Florida. The only real expense would be the airfare. We would even be able to cook our own food and not have to eat out every meal! Our honeymoon was set!

Our honeymoon night was also my responsibility. I knew of a really nice hotel in Peoria area named "Jumers'" I didn't want anyone to know about it. I didn't want any practical jokes that night! I had arranged for my brother, my best man to drive us to the airport and then I would tell him that we were going to honeymoon in Florida. I would give him a paper with an address and phone number where we could be reached in case of an emergency, and then we would say good-bye. Everyone would figure that we needed to catch our plane to Florida then, because the whole wedding day and when we were planning out two receptions, I kept saying, everything's fine as long as we are free by 6:00pm. This led everyone to think our plane was going out that night. So after my brother drove off, I would call up the hotel in the area and ask for their limousine to pick up us and transport us to our hotel for the evening and then the next afternoon, when our plane really WAS leaving for Florida, the limousine took us back to the airport. This kept our honeymoon night a secret and it worked perfectly!

My other responsibility was getting our cabin ready for us to live in for our first 3 months of wedding bliss. This would be our first home and we would live it at camp. I wanted to make sure it was really nice and cozy for Vicki and felt like "our" home. I also wanted it to be away from the rest of the camp activities so we could enjoy peace and privacy. There were some very old, torn up and dirty cabins that hadn't been used by the camp for quite a while and it showed. So I got busy cleaning and fixing this cabin up for my bride in my spare time. I have to say that it looked pretty good by the time I was done. I had it padlocked while I was getting married and on my honeymoon until I unlocked the cabin, our first home and carried my bride over our new threshold. She liked it!

My only other obstacle bcfore my wedding was short but packed summer classes at Trinity College for the last 3 weeks before June. The classes I would take met for about three hours everyday, but it was for only three weeks. This would get an extra six hours of credit in for me and get me closer to our goal of me finishing up Trinity in one semester after we were married. Two days before the wedding I would be done. Time started to tick by quickly. Soon the classes were done, the arrangements were all made, our cabin was completed and I was on my way to Morton for my wedding!

Graduation Day came and all of my family and Jim's family rejoiced! We had a party together at the Smith's house afterwards and then I kissed Jim good-bye as my parents took me home to Morton. The next time I would see Jim in one week, he would be in Morton for our wedding! I had to leave my engagement ring with Jim, because the jeweler was soldered it to the wedding band in preparation for our day. During the next week, I kept feeling my ring finger. It felt so empty, yet then I had an exciting feeling because I knew that soon a WEDDING RING was going to replace it forever!

Speaking of preparations, in one week all the final deci-sions were made ...gifts for people in the wedding party, making small finger sandwiches for our church reception every spare minute and putting them in friend's freezers and gathering decorations for the reception. Also, we were checking out a restaurant for our second reception that we were having for our extended family and out of town guests, which would follow our church reception. More time was spent organizing wedding gifts and packing for the summer at camp (we would be living in a one room cabin for the summer) ,planning for the honeymoon, having a wedding shower and trying to get some REST!! Jim was be the assistant camp director and I would be the secretary to the manager).

Meanwhile, Jim cleaned and prepared our "one room" cabin to bring me home to after our one week Florida honeymoon.. He would bring gifts (like sheets, towels, candles, etc.) from our showers back with him to camp (he worked and lived there for the month of May). I never saw our "one room" cabin until the day he carried me over the threshold as Mrs. James D. Smith. I was amazed, because he had chosen as our cabin an old dirty run down one and transformed it into our first home. It was beautiful and very romantic to have your groom prepare a place for you - kind of like what God is doing for us in heaven - preparing a place just for us, his bride! It was a wonderful gift Jim prepared and gave to me.

Anyway, those were the preparations that Jim and I kept very busy with to pass our time. The next thing I knew it was Thursday night and Jim arrived in Morton in our "new" old car we bought, honking into our driveway, the last time as a single man. The long wait was over and Praise the Lord June 3rd was right around the corner!

Our plans change but God's plans never change. God gives us freedom to move within the boundaries of his plans, like the clothes we wear, the food we eat, the school we go to and even the person we marry. It is like moving around in a fenced in pasture, with very clear boundaries of how far the horses can go. However, there are always limits to our freedom. God's ultimate plan is that we bring him glory and make disciples for him. We should make plans, but always remember that God will make sure the final outcome is for his benefit.

"We can make our plans, but the final outcome is in God's hands." Proverbs 15:1 (LB)

"We may throw the dice, but the LORD determines how they fall." Proverbs 16:33 NIV

"So whether you eat or drink or whatever you do, do it all for the glory of God." 1 Corinthians 10:31

Chapter 20

The Wedding

〜

Most girls have dreamed of their wedding day since they were a little girl playing with dolls. For guys, the honeymoon seems to be the big event to plan, since most of the wedding plans fall into the bride's lap, but regardless who plans what, getting married is a forever moment that has been thought about for a long time. For most weddings, the bride is the star of the day. No one is more important. It is her day. The co-star is not the groom, it is the mother of the bride, followed by the bridesmaids and then perhaps the groom and his side of the family. Thinking about the "big day" can be over-whelming, but don't lose sight of the importance of a wedding. It is the public ceremony that seals the deal. It is a promise, a commitment to someone else for the rest of your life in the sight of God and all those guests. It is a joyous day that should be one of the most exciting days of your lifetime. Remember to celebrate your love for each other not only this day, but for a lifetime. God told the Israelites to remember His faithfulness and goodness to them throughout every year, and we should do the same by remembering birthdays, holidays and especially, anniversaries.

The wedding day takes a lot of planning, but one never knows how it will really turn out. However, the bride and groom should concentrate also on what really happens on that day. It really isn't all about the other people, the music, the food, the flowers, the decorations, or the weather. It is about the sincere and solemn promise to live for God and one another. You stand in front of God and your closest witnesses and promise to give up your dreams, desires and comforts for only this one. You have taken on the responsibility of caring for this person for the rest of your life, no matter what. God gives you instructions on how to care for and live with your husband and wife and so from the wedding on, you need to obey them and fulfill the other person. Take care of them the way God has instructed, with love and commitment not, on how you feel or if you think you CAN do it

It is well worth the wait...

I had heard that after you marry that you soon wake up and panic, realizing just what you have done. Commitment is for a lifetime to just one other person. I never had that thought, and I was looking forward to spending the rest of my life with my best friend. Vicki truly was the best friend I had, my special friend given to me by God. She was my accountability friend, my encouraging friend and she even enjoyed watching football games with me. Marriage will intensify everything you have in a relationship, and I was not afraid to double anything. Joys are doubled and burdens are halved, and there was no cold feet in my thinking. The big day was here, the long awaited wedding, followed by our honeymoon. I guess it is safe to say that I thought much more about our honeymoon than I did about our wedding, and I am sure Vicki thought more about our wedding than our honeymoon. We both worked on what we thought about the most. She did most of the planning for the wedding, and I did most of the planning of the honeymoon. Soon we would be man and wife and sex would be a God encouraged part of our marriage. All my life I was told to wait, and now it was soon going to be no longer forbidden. I was glad I waited and that I was a virgin, as was Vicki. We could give each other a gift of purity, that would only cause us to trust each other throughout our marriage. If you wait for sex until after marriage, the chances are better that you will remain faithful to your spouse during your marriage. Suddenly, like graduation, I would be entering a new world of responsibility and enjoyment.

A tuxedo rental place had asked us if they could film portions of our reception to use for a TV commercial in the Peoria area. I, and my best man would get our tuxedo's free and most everyone else would get a very good discount. Vicki had chosen to go with a rainbow of pastel colors for our June wedding, and so each groomsman would have a different colored shirt to go with our white tuxedo's. We agreed to let them film part of the reception, and we even got one dollar for payment. Ha!

By Friday, the day before our wedding, all the groomsmen who were Jim's friends had arrived, so to keep them busy and because most of them hadn't seen each other since their Moody graduation, they all went out golfing with my dad. My mom, who was an elementary teacher offered to stay home and help me with last moment tasks, but I knew all the running I needed to do. I thanked her for her kind offer, but I thought a little time alone would be good and I could rush around easier by myself. I would be focused and get every-thing done. I had my list, my parent's car, and time so after a quick breakfast, I was off and running. My list was being completed, but moment by moment, my right eye would hurt more and more. By the time that Jim and the groomsmen had finished golfing and came to the church to help me set up for the reception, I was in extreme pain. When I saw Jim and my dad, I ran over to them and began to cry. I was in terrible pain. My dad called the eye doctor and informed him of the circumstances.

Jim drove me and on the way there, I was upset. It was already 3:00 PM and our rehearsal was scheduled at the church for 4:00 PM. Everyone would be there. Jim comforted me and said as long as the main two, the bride and groom, weren't there everyone else would wait! We needed to get help for my eye right now and not worry about the rehearsal. As we drove and waited in the doctor's office, I calmed down and actually Jim and I caught up with what we had been doing all day, and how we were feeling on this day before our wedding. It was some "alone" time before the busy day. The doctor said my right contact had cut my eye, so he gave me some eye drop medication and said I probably couldn't wear my contacts for the next 4-6 weeks while my eye recovered. The medication would just help it to feel better. I really didn't care about the next 4-6 weeks, just tomorrow! What would I do if I couldn't wear my contacts? My choices were to wear my glasses or wear one contact in my left eye and try to half way see my wedding, or to wear no contacts or glasses and not see my wedding at all that I had that I had been planning for the last 17 months!

However, with God, there is ALWAYS another option... ALWAYS the BEST option. Jim and I and all my wedding party decided to pray that if God would allow it, to let me wear my contacts for at least the one hour of the next day, so I could see the ceremony. God said "Yes", and the next morning, I put my right contact on my right eye and wore it ALL day without any pain! However, for the next 4 weeks I could NEVER put it in my eye because of the pain. Thank you Lord for what some call "little miracles". For some people this was not a big deal, but for me it was amazing and a special gift from my Heavenly Father for my day.

Our rehearsal night, we came to our "postponed" reception, with a patch over my right eye. It was thrilling to have all our family and many friends there who supported our union. Jim and I introduced everyone and we practiced everything. I realized by the end of the rehearsal that I was not only the coordinator of this great event, but also the "star"!

The Smith's decided to have a big picnic at a park in our town. This was a great idea because first of all we had a huge wedding party - 6 bridesmaids, 6 groomsmen, 4 ushers, 2 flower girls, 2 pastors, 2 singers, musicians and all their families and then our extended families that were all invited also since most had come from out of town and there really wasn't a restaurant who could hold them all and the bill would be too much. Kentucky Fried Chicken was served for all and we all talked on the picnic tables and played Frisbee football. It was a relaxing night and gave people a chance to talk to both Jim and me and then meet new people or reacquaint with one another in a very casual atmosphere. It almost seemed as if we were just at a big family reunion.

We got the tux's and then onto the wedding rehearsal. I had just arrived in town on Thursday and the rehearsal was the next day at 4pm. Vicki and I went to her eye doctor, because her eye started to swell up, which caused us to stay a little longer at the doctor, which in turn got us to the church much later than the scheduled time. The good thing was that they couldn't start the rehearsal without us! I remember having to introduce all our groomsmen and bridesmaids, plus parents and relatives to everyone, realizing that Vicki and I were the only two who knew everyone there. Vicki's Uncle Bob would do the vows and we had to decide what names we wanted to use, James & Victoria, or Jim & Vicki or mix them up. We decided to go formal, James & Victoria. Our napkins even had James & Victoria and they were the true names on our birth certificates that our parents had formally named us.

We had a picnic afterwards for our rehearsal dinner at a park outside of Morton. That was fun! A chance to talk with one another in a casual manner and then the guys went off and played Frisbee football, while the others watched and talked around the picnic tables.

My groomsmen, ushers and I spent the night at some of my future in-law's friend's home. The woman gave us her whole upstairs and so we had fun the last night of my life as a bachelor. I called Vicki that night around midnight and mentioned to her that the next time I would see her would be when she came down the aisle in our wedding. We wanted to take our pictures afterwards so we wouldn't see each other before the wedding ceremony and we wouldn't have to take our pictures too early in the morning, seeing as our ceremony was to be at 11:00am. Anticipation was the name of this game. As I went to bed that night I still remember thinking that tomorrow night, Vicki and I will be in the same bed together and it will all be right. Life, if lived God's way, has it's rewards, even here on earth.

I went home, packed up a few things for my honeymoon and all of a sudden realized, "I'm going on a vacation tomorrow for a week in Florida." That was a fun thought. I'd be going to Florida as Mrs. James D. Smith. After I was ready for bed, a phone call came around midnight. It was my groom and he tenderly reminded me that the next time he would see me would be at the other end of the aisle and he also said that this would be the last day he would be talking to me as Vicki Sutter - tomorrow I would become Vicki Smith. Tomorrow was the day we had prayed and waited for, for 17 months. I slept very well after this, my heart in perfect peace and awoke to a beautiful June morning.

Jim and I had decided upon a 11:00 am wedding, primarily so that Jim's pastor and many friends from his church could easily come to our wedding and return home in the same day. They lived about 3 hours away, so it made a full day, but they wouldn't have to return home too late. Jim and I had been very involved with Moody church as youth sponsors and with the camp, and Jim's father was an associate pastor there, so many people did come to attend our wedding. Another reason for the 11:00 am wedding time was because we were having 2 receptions - one general reception with all the small finger sandwiches, relishes and the bridal cake which was for everyone and a second smaller reception at a restaurant for family members and very close friends who had traveled far. The restaurant had a buffet and Jim and I loved to be with all our families. We also needed to open ALL our wedding presents during this reception, since we were going straight to our camp positions after our honeymoon. The presents needed to be opened and recorded so we could write the thank you notes. Another advantage to a setting an 11 am time for your wedding, is that you don't have to sit around and get nervous all day.

I got up, had my devotions, ate a little breakfast, went to the hairdressers and came home to realize I had nothing to wear over to the church where my wedding dress was hanging up. I only had the old "out of style" clothes after all the sorting out and packing between college and moving etc. I had to dig out some of my old "high school
day" clothes out of my closet in order to get over to the church. Oh well in about an hour, I would be wearing the most beautiful dress in the world.

Being a bride is the most special feeling. It was so right and so exciting. I was ready to leave my goals, my dreams, and choose his goals, his dreams which really had become "our" goals, "our" dreams.

The day had arrived. It was a great day. The sun was shining and the temperature was just perfect. Our 11:00 am wedding didn't allow much time for anything else except to get up and get ready. Since my groomsmen and I were staying at the same place we all joked around the entire morning. We arrived at the church together around 10 am for pictures that would not involve Vicki and me together, like one of me, one with me and my folks, one of me with Vicki's folks, me and my groomsmen alone, me and ....., well you get the idea. Then as the clock ticked ever so quickly toward 11:00 am, Steve reminded all of us to put our right hand over our left hand, as we stood in the front. This was important to my brother Dan and me, because we were the only ones in the front of the church. All the others were coming up as couples down the middle aisle. We had a time of prayer and then the big event in my life was about to begin.

I was glad I had been involved in a men's singing group at Moody, because then I had a little experience in front to of crowds, but I was still very nervous about this wedding. It wasn't about getting married that made me nervous, but it was about getting in front of all those people and having to talk. The organ began and the pastors mentioned to Dan and I that it was time to go. Wow, look at all the people I didn't even know. I didn't look at them long, since I had to find my place on the platform and place my right hand over my left, or was it left over the right? I glanced over at Dan and did what he did!

All the couples came walking up the aisle towards us. I smiled and really thought they looked nice with their matching dress and shirt. This was the first time I had really paid attention to the dresses and was glad that Vicki had done such a nice job of planning. I also kept looking at my friends, because I didn't want to think about all those people here and possibly faint. Yes, that wouldn't go over real well. Finally I saw Vicki and her dad getting ready in the back.

Dan had moved up the platform and I was now all alone on looking at my bride coming down the aisle. My song that I wanted started to play and all stood to face Vicki. I too was looking at her and I was glad I was marrying her. She looked so beautiful. She looked at me, but then she also looked at everyone else standing by the aisle. It almost looked like she stopped and talked to everyone coming down the aisle, but finally she arrived at the front. Our eyes met, we were ready. A prayer was given and the ceremony began.

My mind went suddenly blank and I didn't remember anything. I knew Vicki would remember, so I followed her every move. When the pastor did the vows, I panicked, thinking I would forget a line or something. "And hereto I pledge my faithfulness" was the longest sentence in the world to me at that time. Then I was asked, "What token of your love do you have to give to Victoria at this time?" I had no idea what the pastor was talking about. After what seemed to be a lifetime, which was really only one or two seconds, I remembered and got the ring from my best man. Of course the ring had a thread tied to it, but fortunately it broke as I took the ring. Then, since these guys tried that joke, during our prayer of dedication I was worried that they had written H-E-L-P on the bottoms of my shoes. They didn't. Then I was told that I could kiss my bride. During the whole ceremony I never knew when I was supposed to kiss Vicki. During every pause I turned towards her so I was ready. We kissed and then I knew the ceremony was almost done. I was married. Through the long journey of life I was now to have a companion.

"I now present to you, Mr. and Mrs. James D. Smith!" I think we ran down the aisle and hugged and kissed in the lobby. We were officially married!

Every detail of our wedding had been pondered over and planned and it was thrilling to watch the whole day unfold. Our decor was ALL in pastels so each couple presented a different paste colorl with their gowns and dress shirts. The best man and maid of honor wore light green, as did the 2 flower girls, who were our two little sisters, ages 10 and 5 at the time. The second couple wore yellow, the third peach, the fourth lavender, the fifth pink and the sixth couple wore light blue. Each bridesmaid carried a bouquet of daisies tinted the same pastel color which they were wearing and the flower girls had baskets of multi-colored pastel petals which decorated the aisle.

We had a wonderful organist, a superb violinist, and two talented singers who all performed to their potential and filled our ceremony with beautiful music.

As I took my dad's arm I saw the tear, yet pride in his eye. He didn't need to say a word. I knew he loved me and had done his job well of providing and protecting me up until this moment. He was confidently passing me on to a man whom he knew would keep his vows to cherish, provide and protect his daughter all his life. I loved "my daddy" and was thankful to be led down the aisle by this Godly loving man. As I entered the church sanctuary, I was overwhelmed at ALL the people who came from so many places geographically and so many places from my life and Jim's life. Jim said he didn't know if I would stop greeting people and make it down the aisle, but we finally did and our eyes met. This was it! I was being presented to my groom, standing firmly and confidently, looking at me with eye of anticipation and adoration. This was not a scary moment, it was sacred and long awaited and joyful.

"Who gives this woman to this man?"

"Her mother and I."

I then let go of my "daddy" and reached for Jim's strong arm and the touch sent shivers down my spine. I was about to enter his life forever.

"Let us pray."
"This is the day the Lord has made, we will rejoice and be glad in it."
Yes we had rejoiced, we were rejoicing right this moment and we will be rejoicing every day in which God gives us!

The honeymoon, children, adventures and storms would come our way, but with Christ, we would face them together.
"What God hath joined together, let no man separate." We would take this bond seriously and joyously. When life is done and the sun is setting, we would be found then as now, still hand in hand, still thanking God for each other until we lay the other into the arms of God.

I had writtten a song for Jim that day which I sang to him at our reception. Here are the words td that song and the "feelings" of my heart as that day approached. I finished this song just days before our wedding.

"This is the day that the Lord has made.
We will rejoice and be glad in it.
For we believe, God has given us
A gift of His great love for us.
For He has led us to this special special day,
and He will continue to lead us ..in the days to come.

We will seek first your kingdom, dear Lord,
And we know that all these things will be added unto us.
For we want you to be the Head,
The Head of our new home.
We'll serve you, glorify you, through our lives together,
We'll love you, magnify you through our home together
    Lord.

I have waited and prayed for you so long.
You are my man of faith and patience, just what I
asked for.
For I believe God has given me
A gift of His great love for me.
This gift of love is you My Beloved,
My Beloved, My Husband sent to me from our Lord."

We had remained pure,
we had honored our parents, and trusted God's
plans for this day instead of our own desires.
We had worked hard and put our faith
and trust in God's hands. We were ready
to serve the Lord together as friends for
the rest our lifetimes. FOREVER FRIENDS.
We give praise to our Lord forever.

"Two are better than one, because they have a good
return for their work." Ecc. 4:9 NIV

Printed in the United States
72153LV00002B/65